THE
HEIDELBERG CATECHISM

THE
HEIDELBERG CATECHISM

A STUDY GUIDE

G. I. Williamson

P&R
PUBLISHING
P.O. BOX 817 • PHILLIPSBURG • NEW JERSEY 08865

The text of the Heidelberg Catechism is from the *Psalter Hymnal,* 1959 edition. Used by permission of CRC Publications. Scripture quotations within that edition of the Catechism are from the American Standard Edition of the Revised Bible, © 1929, the International Council of Religious Education.

Unless otherwise indicated, Scripture quotations within the commentary portion of this volume are from The New King James Version. Copyright © 1979, 1980, 1982, Thomas Nelson, Inc.

Questions for Study and Discussion at the end of each chapter have been graciously contributed by Bruce Hoyt.

Manufactured in the United States of America.

Library of Congress Cataloging-in-Publication Data

Williamson, G. I. (Gerald Irvin), 1925–
    The Heidelberg catechism : a study guide / G. I. Williamson.
        p.   cm.
    Includes the entire text of the catechism in English.
    Includes index.
    ISBN-10: 0–87552–551–2
    ISBN-13: 978-0–87552–551–8
    1. Heidelberger Katechismus. I. Heidelberger Katechismus. English.
1993. II. Title.
BX9428.W55 1993
238'.42—dc20   93–36201

To

Dick G. Vanderpyl

An Elder who never stopped growing.

CONTENTS

FOREWORD

Looming over the river Neckar, and watching over the ancient city, is the great castle of Heidelberg, once the seat of Elector Frederick III. It was here in ancient Heidelberg that the Lord long ago began a great work of reformation in the hearts of the people and their rulers. Lasting testimony of this fact is the so-called Heidelberg Catechism, commissioned by Frederick III himself not long after his accession in 1559, to be a proclamation of the biblical faith to the world.

But the great castle in Heidelberg did not prove the fortress it appeared to be. Heidelberg was sacked and occupied several times during the Thirty Years' War. The castle itself often fell prey to ravaging fire. The moat leaked badly and was in fact never able to be filled. Today there is not much left of the castle, or of the Reformation in Heidelberg. Tours of the ancient city and castle ruins are available, but not one word is spoken of its role in the Reformation. A question directed about the Heidelberg Catechism itself is more likely to leave the tour-guide with a blank unknowing expression.

Yet praise be to our Lord that the labor of the Reformation in Heidelberg has not been completely lost to us. The Catechism, transported to the Netherlands, took root and, since its inception, has become itself a dearly loved guide for generations of Reformed people. But the Catechism doesn't present a tour of ancient ruins. It maps out for the believer the path of salvation revealed in the Scriptures, demonstrating the love of God for a fallen world.

Traditionally the writing of this Catechism has been ascribed to Caspar Olevianus and Zacharias Ursinus. Yet further research in this century has shown that Ursinus alone should be considered the major contributor. Olevianus had no more input in its production than the other theologians and pastors of Heidelberg (i.e., to check it over). Although most of the debate has been in German, a good English summary of the discussion can be found in Frederick H. Klooster's article "The Priority of Ursinus in the Composition of the Heidelberg Catechism," in *Controversy and Conciliation: The Reformation and the Palatinate 1559–1583,* ed. Derk Visser (Allison Park, Pa: Pickwick, 1986). Such research in identifying both the major contributor and his sources has been helpful in understanding the background to our Catechism. It now leaves only the desire that more of the theological works of Ursinus would be translated and published, particularly his *Apologia Catechismi* (*Defense of the Catechism*), written in 1564 to defend the doctrine of the Catechism against various attacks. A new edition of Ursinus's commentary on the Catechism is also long overdue. While that of G. W. Williard (first published 1851, reprinted by Presbyterian and Reformed) can be most helpful, yet his translation is unfortunately often rather inaccurate, sometimes even leading to serious misunderstanding.

Although there is still a need for scholarly historical study of the Catechism, this cannot be said for the equally necessary study guide for the churches. G. I. Williamson has once again done the church an invaluable service by providing this study on the Heidelberg Catechism. In simple and clear language he has opened up the wealth of the Catechism for all to see. G. I.'s long experience as a teacher of catechism has given him the expertise and wisdom that make his study guides so successful. As a former pupil of his I can personally vouch for his dedication to this method of teaching. For that, I myself shall be eternally grateful. When G. I. asked me to write a foreword for this volume, I was only too pleased to oblige. It is my prayer that the Lord will bless its use throughout his churches for the upbuilding of his people.

The value of the Heidelberg Catechism is not restricted to any one age or people, but insofar as it maps the saving doctrines of the Scriptures, it will continue to be used with profit the world over. Perhaps the best way of showing its timeless value is to read once again the introduction attached to the first editions (see the following). I can think of no better introduction to the Catechism or its use.

R. Dean Anderson, Jr.

Original Introduction to the Heidelberg Catechism

"A catechism in our Christian Religion" is the name given to a brief and simple orally given summary of the main parts of Christian doctrine in which the youth and beginners are examined and heard on what they have learned. For from the beginning of the Christian church all the godly have been diligent to instruct their children in the fear of the Lord, at home, at school and in church. They did so undoubtedly for the following reasons which shall induce us also to do the same.

In the first place they rightly took into consideration the fact that inborn wickedness would get the upper hand and then pervert churches and civil governments unless it were countered in time by means of salutary doctrine.

In the second place they had the express command of God in Exod 12 and 13 and in Deut 4, 6, and 11 where the Lord says "and these words (the 10 commandments) which I command you this day shall be upon your heart and you shall teach them diligently to your children and shall talk of them when you sit in your house, and when you walk by the way, and when you lie down and when you rise up."

Finally just as the children of Israel, after circumcision and as soon as they were able to understand, were instructed in the mystery of this covenant sign, and also in the covenant of God, so our children too are to be instructed in the significance of baptism which they have received, and in the true Christian faith and repentance, in order that before they are admitted to the Lord's table they may profess their faith before the whole Christian congregation.

The Catechism must therefore
be maintained according
to the following form.

Firstly, since the older people under the papacy were educated without catechism and easily forget the parts of the Christian religion, it is deemed necessary that the minister read a section of the catechism to the people clearly and understandably before the sermon on each Sunday and on all festive days. This is to be done in the villages and towns as well as the cities so that it is completed on nine Sundays. [There follows a division of the Catechism into nine Sundays]

Further, every Sunday afternoon at a convenient time a catechism sermon shall be delivered in the following manner. After the congregation has finished singing the minister shall first repeat the Lord's Prayer and call upon God for a right understanding of his Word, and then clearly read the 10 commandments to the people. After that he shall examine those who have not yet been able to learn the questions on which he will preach, and in an orderly fashion instruct them, first for some time on the text and thereafter step by step through the subject matter. After this let him make some of the youth recite a certain number of the questions in the catechism (which for this purpose we divided into Lord's Days), both those preceding and especially those to come next Sunday, which they have learnt before at school or at home. As soon as they have completed reciting them in the presence of the congregation, the minister shall simply and briefly interpret and explain a small number of the following questions so that he may complete the catechism preaching at least once every year.

INTRODUCTION

SCRIPTURE READINGS: *Luke 1:1–4;*
Deuteronomy 26:1–11; 1 Timothy 3:14–16

The Heidelberg Catechism is one of the finest creeds of the Reformation period. A faithful teacher of millions, it has stood the test of time. It is still, today, one of the best tools available for learning what it means to be a Christian.

As the name suggests, the Heidelberg Catechism originated in Germany. Frederick III, the regional ruler who lived in Heidelberg in the time of the Reformation, wanted a better manual for religious instruction for his people. The result was a catechism written primarily by Zacharius Ursinus and named after the city of its origin. It was published in 1563 and was quickly—and widely—accepted.

In the third edition the Catechism was arranged under 52 divisions to correspond to the number of weeks in the year. And from that time to this, in many Reformed churches, pastors make use of this Catechism to unfold the biblical system of doctrine. The Catechism was soon translated into the Dutch language and has perhaps been loved in no other part of the church more than in the Netherlands. It has been widely accepted in many other parts of the world, however, and remains one of the most widely studied summaries of the Christian faith.

But why study a creed? Wouldn't it be better to study just the Bible? After all, creeds are manmade. The Bible is divinely inspired. Do we not dishonor God's Word if we study a catechism? This is a common conception. You even find churches today with slogans such as "No creed but the Bible." Yet the truth is that the Bible itself contradicts such thinking. We can see this very clearly from the opening words of Luke's gospel:

Inasmuch as many have taken in hand to set in order a narrative of those things which are most surely believed among us, just as those who from the beginning were eyewitnesses and ministers of the word delivered them to us, it seemed good to me also, having had perfect understanding of all things from the very first, to write to you an orderly account, most excellent Theophilus, that you may know the certainty of those things in which you were instructed [or "catechized," in the Greek]. (Luke 1:1–4)

So Theophilus did not just begin with his own study of the Bible. No, he began (as we all do) by receiving instruction from others. He was catechized, in other words, and then went on to test and confirm his catechism lessons by his own study of Scripture. Notice that Luke did not regard catechetical teaching, by itself, as sufficient. No, he wanted Theophilus to *"know the certainty of those things in which [he had been] instructed."* So the test of truth is the Bible, not the Catechism. We must always go from the Catechism to the Bible in order to make sure that it teaches the truth.

LIKE A MAP

You see, then, that the Catechism is something like a map. We could ask, "Why bother to study a map? Why not just go out and study the surface of the earth instead?" The answer, of course, is that one is wise to begin with a study of maps. After all, life is short and the world is very big. One person, working by himself, could only map a small portion of the earth's surface. That is why maps are so valuable. They exist because many people over many years have made a study of the earth. And while these maps are not perfect, they are quite accurate. Thus, the best way to begin to understand the geography of the world is not to start with the world itself. No, the best way is to start with a good atlas. Then, after getting hold of the basics, one can go out and test the atlas by actually visiting some of the places described in it.

It is much the same with the Bible. The Bible contains a great wealth of information. It isn't easy to master it all—in fact, no one has ever mastered it completely. It would therefore be foolish for us to try to do it on our own, starting from scratch. We would be ignoring all the study of the Word of God that other people have done down through the centuries. That is exactly why we have creeds. They are the product of many centuries of Bible study by a great company of believers. They are a kind of spiritual "road map" of the teaching of the Bible, already worked out and proved by others before us. And, after all, isn't this exactly what Jesus promised? When he was about to finish his work on earth, he made this promise to his disciples: *"When He, the Spirit of truth, has come, He will guide you into all truth"* (John 16:13). And Christ kept his promise. When the Day of Pentecost came, he sent his Spirit to dwell in his people. The Holy Spirit was poured out—not on individuals, each by himself, but on the whole body of Christian believers together (Acts 2). And from that time until this, he has been giving his church an understanding of the Scriptures. It is no wonder that the church expressed itself from very early times through creeds.

A LINK WITH THE PAST

One of the unique things about the Heidelberg Catechism is that it really is two creeds in one. Or, to say it differently, there is a creed within this creed. You see, a large part of this catechism (or creed) is simply a careful explanation of the Apostles' Creed. The Apostles' Creed is the earliest, or most ancient, creed of the church. And right here we see one of the most important things about a creed that is true to the Bible—it remains true down through the ages. It does not need to be changed again and again, with each generation, because it deals with things that are unchanging. Thus, an accurate creed binds the generations together. It reminds us that the church of Jesus Christ is not confined to one age, just as it is not confined to any one place. In other words, there is a unity in what Christians have believed, right down through the ages. Just think of it: when we confess our faith today in the words of the Apostles' Creed, we join with all those believers who have gone before us. Does this not demonstrate that there is indeed just one Lord and one true faith?

It will be our purpose in these studies of the Heidelberg Catechism to show this again and again, by going back to the Scriptures. Our starting point will be the Catechism, but our final reference point will be the Bible. Only when we are sure that the Catechism agrees with the Word of God will we have the kind of certainty that Luke recommended to Theophilus. It will be clear from this that we must never regard the

Catechism as equal with the Bible. If my atlas says something that does not agree with what I actually find on the surface of the earth, I will not say, "The world is out of line with my atlas." No, it will be the atlas that needs correction, not the world. So it is with all creeds and confessions. We may never regard them in the same way that we regard the Bible. If the creed is out of line with the Bible at any point, we must be willing to admit it. But a wise person will be careful. He will first want to check and recheck before reaching this conclusion. The Heidelberg Catechism has been tested many times by many Christian believers who have found it true to the Scriptures. It is our hope that in these studies we can show why we firmly agree with their conclusion.

QUESTIONS ON THE LESSON

1. Explain why it is wise to begin learning the Christian faith by using a catechism.
2. How is a catechism similar to a road map?
3. What creed is explained in the Heidelberg Catechism?
4. Show from Luke 1:1–4 where we are to find our ultimate authority.

QUESTIONS FOR STUDY AND DISCUSSION

1. What serious dangers exist for churches that reject the use of creeds?
2. Why is it necessary for every church to have a creed (perhaps an unwritten one), even though it claims not to have one? What happens when someone in the church teaches error?
3. If God wanted us to use creeds, why didn't he attach one on the end of the Bible? (Hint: How do creeds function in the church?)
4. Many people get bogged down reading the Bible because they don't understand its overall structure and don't know its basic teachings. How will the study of a creed alleviate this difficulty?

LORD'S DAY 1

SCRIPTURE READINGS: *Genesis 1–11;*
Hebrews 2:14–18; Titus 2:11–14

The Heidelberg Catechism consists of a series of 129 questions and answers. These are arranged according to a plan. The first two questions and answers are introductory. Then follow three major parts: the first (Q/A 3–11) deals with man's sin and misery; the second (Q/A 12–85) shows the way of deliverance; and the third (Q/A 86–129) unfolds the life of gratitude that is to be expected in those who are saved. In the remainder of this section we will deal with the introductory questions and answers.

1. Q. **What is your only comfort in life and death?**
    A. That I, with body and soul, both in life and death, am not my own, but belong unto my faithful Savior Jesus Christ; who with His precious blood has fully satisfied for all my sins, and delivered me from all the power of the devil; and so preserves me that without the will of my heavenly Father not a hair can fall from my head; yea, that all things must be subservient to my salvation, wherefore by His Holy Spirit He also assures me of eternal life, and makes me heartily willing and ready, henceforth, to live unto Him.

2. Q. **How many things are necessary for you to know, that you in this comfort may live and die happily?**
    A. Three; the first, how great my sins and misery are; the second, how I am delivered from all my sins and misery; the third, how I am to be thankful to God for such deliverance.

The Catechism begins with a question that is very important to every one of us. Whether we realize it or not, we need comfort. We need comfort because we are descendants of Adam and Eve. Being their descendants, we are (even if we are ignorant of it) in a condition of sin and misery.

If we go back to the early chapters of the Bible (chaps. 1–6 of Gen.), we read about the creation of man and then about man's fall into sin. When Adam and Eve sinned against God, profound changes occurred. God drove them out of the Garden of Eden. They became sinful in character. Sin multiplied in the world. There began to be crime and lawlessness.

The world became a dangerous place. And, in the end, whether from violence, disease, or old age, people all finally died. In other words, in just the first six chapters of the Bible, God tells us that we lost something like "heaven on earth" (in the Garden of Eden) and found ourselves in a world that began to resemble hell. We will never understand the truth about ourselves unless we take full account of what has happened. The world of today is better, in some ways, than the world was before the great Flood that finally came in Noah's day. The reason for this is that God has given some things to mankind since that time, to restrain the power of evil on earth and to moderate the misery that issues from it. For one thing, God divided the human race by causing people to speak different languages (Gen. 11).

Because of this, there is now no complete unity in the development of evil. Different nations tend to compete in different power groups, the one against the other, instead of uniting in evil. God has also put the power of the sword in the hands of civil rulers in order to restrain men in the evil they would otherwise do. It is for this reason that we have police forces and national armies and navies to deter aggression. God uses these things to restrain and limit the development of evil. And then, last but not least, God has instituted the church in the midst of the world, but distinct from it. When the church is faithful to God's holy Word, it also does much to retard the development of evil. For reasons such as these, the world is not as bad today as it was before the Flood. The first few chapters of Genesis are so very important because they teach us what happened in that period of history before God introduced these changes into the world.

At first, God permitted evil to develop to the full, we could say, so that all people in subsequent ages might know how great man's sin and misery really are. And while we today can be very thankful that sin is somewhat restrained in the world, we also need to realize—from this scriptural data—that our human predicament is still basically a desperate one. Just stop and think of the millions of people killed in war. Think of all who have been persecuted and tortured. Think of all the suffering endured because of diseases. Think of all the crime and misery that result from it. Think of what misery it must be to spend a lifetime in prison.

These are sad realities in the world in which we are living. But they are only some of the more obvious things. Take a small town, for instance. On the surface, things may look very peaceful and pleasant. But if we knew all about the people who live there, we would soon discover serious problems in almost every household. Here is a young widow, grief-stricken because her husband was recently killed. A few doors away you have a father and mother distressed because their little infant was born with a serious abnormality. Another household is torn apart by strife between husband and wife. Still another is in great turmoil because of rebellious teenage children.

Is it any wonder that the Catechism—following the Bible—speaks of our sin and misery as it does? Yes, the truth is that our human predicament is tragic.

Yet the amazing thing is that so many people are unwilling to admit it. As a matter of fact, they do many things to keep from facing the unpleasant truth. They get drunk. They go to parties. They take drugs. They escape into the fantasy world of TV. Yet none of these diversions can change the unpleasant facts.

So our number-one need is finally to face up to our real situation—and then find the solution. That is why the Catechism says in Answer 2 that we must come to know three things if we are ever to find the solution. The first thing we need to know is the unpleasant truth about our tragic situation. Once we understand this, we can go on to learn that there is indeed a solution. The solution is the saving work accomplished by the Lord Jesus.

Now all of this is clearly stated in Q/A 2 of the Heidelberg Catechism. Here we have a comprehensive outline of the whole Catechism. This will become clear as we proceed. But first let us note that we also have—in Q/A 1—a kind of summary of everything that follows. You see, by asking "What is your only comfort?" the Catechism already makes an assumption. The assumption is that we are miserable sinners and therefore need to find comfort. And the way we can find comfort is summarized right here in this first answer. The finished work of the Lord Jesus Christ provides exactly the comfort we need. And when we get possession of that, we will certainly be thankful for it, so much so that then we will want to live for Jesus.

Let us put it this way: What is it that makes one a Christian? Is it not the simple fact that the Christian has genuine comfort (as distinct from the many counterfeits that we see around us today)? And what is this comfort?

The answer is found in two things: what Jesus has already done for me, and what he continues to do for me. We will deal with these in greater detail later on. For now, we just want briefly to state what they are. The work that Christ has already done for me is this: He paid the price of my sin. As long as that price was not paid, I belonged to Satan. But once it was paid in full, I was no longer under Satan's control. The Bible puts it like this: *"Inasmuch then as the children have partaken of flesh and blood, He Himself likewise shared in the same, that through death He might destroy him who had the power of death, that is, the devil, and release those who through fear of death were all their lifetime subject to bondage"* (Heb. 2:14–15). Christ satisfied the demands of the justice of God in order to effect this deliverance.

But there is also much that Jesus does now on behalf of his people. He exercises all authority over all things in heaven and on earth (Matt. 28:18–20). And because *"the Lord is faithful,"* he *"will establish you and guard you from the evil one"* (2 Thess. 3:3). He does this by controlling everything in the world around us and through the power of his Holy Spirit dwelling within us.

So the misery of man is great. But the work of Jesus Christ is still greater. In the midst of sorrow I can therefore rejoice. I can do this because I belong—body and soul, now and forever—to Jesus my Savior. He promised to share his inheritance with his people. This inheritance includes many things—too many to mention here—but there is one thing that must be mentioned, namely, death. As we shall see later on in these studies, Christ has conquered death. Because of this, although it is appointed to men once to die, even in death the sting is removed for believers. It does not have the power to hurt us as it can—and does—hurt those who do not have Jesus as their Savior. And when our Lord returns at the end of this age, death itself will be destroyed as he raises us up from the grave to share in his glory. The outlook, in other words, is for a complete deliverance from all sin and from all the effects it has brought upon us. Is it any wonder that one who is given so great a salvation becomes "heartily willing and ready, henceforth, to live" for such a Redeemer? How could we do otherwise?

May God enable you to see this and experience it as you continue to listen to the lessons taught by this venerable teacher called the Heidelberg Catechism.

QUESTIONS ON THE LESSON

1. What do the three major sections of the Heidelberg Catechism deal with?
2. How is each of these three major sections implied in Q/A 1 of the Catechism?
3. Why is comfort one of our deepest needs?
4. What are some of the things that people today substitute for true comfort?
5. Why does the Christian (alone) have true comfort?

QUESTIONS FOR STUDY AND DISCUSSION

1. Many people today abhor the idea of belonging to someone. Do you think that it is good to belong to someone? To whom?
2. Do you think that God really controls *everything* that happens?
3. Is eternal life an empty religious concept?
4. Is the Devil real—or just a personification of evil?
5. Why should anyone want to live "heartily" for Jesus Christ?

PART I

SIN AND MISERY

LORD'S DAY 2

SCRIPTURE READINGS: *Deuteronomy 5:6–21;*
Romans 7:7–12; Matthew 22:34–40

3.   **Q. Whence do you know your misery?**
      A. Out of the law of God.

4.   **Q. What does the law of God require of us?**
      A. Christ teaches that in a summary, Matt. 22:37–40, *Thou*
      shalt love the Lord thy God with all thy heart, and with all thy
      soul, and with all thy mind. This is the great and first com-
      mandment. And a second like unto it is this, Thou shalt love
      thy neighbor as thyself. On these two commandments the whole
      law hangeth, and the prophets.

5.   **Q. Can you keep all this perfectly?**
      A. In no wise; for I am prone by nature to hate God and my
      neighbor.

Can you imagine what it was like on August 6, 1945, in the city of Hi-
roshima? An American bomber was on its way to drop the atomic bomb.
But the people walking around in the city that day were oblivious to
any such danger. They were about to be destroyed—or at least horribly
disfigured—and yet the sad fact is that they were not aware of the peril.
Their position was desperate (the bomb was soon to fall upon them),
and so was their condition (they were ignorant of the danger).

     This is something like our fallen position—and condition—as we
face the coming judgment of God. The Bible says we are under the wrath
of God by nature. Judgment and eternal damnation are surely coming.

Yet the tragedy is that many people do not realize this as they should. That is why God gave us his law in the Bible. He gave us his law to bring us to see how desperate our position—and condition—really are. You can see this clearly in a statement that Paul made about himself: *"I would not have known sin except through the law. For I would not have known covetousness unless the law had said, 'You shall not covet'"* (Rom. 7:7). What Paul is saying is that he did not realize how desperate his position—and condition—were before God until the law made him see it.

Now this does not mean that people who are without the law written in the Bible are entirely devoid of any awareness that they are sinners. No, the Bible clearly teaches that everyone has at least some awareness of being a sinner and of being under God's wrath and curse. As the Scripture says: *"When Gentiles, who do not have the law, by nature do the things contained in the law, these, although not having the law, are a law to themselves, who show the work of the law written in their hearts, their conscience also bearing witness, and between themselves their thoughts accusing or else excusing them"* (Rom. 2:14–15).

In other words, even people who lack the Bible have some awareness that they are sinners. They realize, to some extent at least, that they have reason to fear God. But note that we say "to some extent." We say this because one of the effects of sin is to weaken this voice of conscience. The more people sin, the more their hearts are hardened. The result is that the voice of conscience is weakened. For this reason, conscience alone is not enough to wake people up to their peril. No, says Paul, *"I would not have known sin except through the law"* (Rom. 7:7). Paul was a Jew. This means that he was born to privilege. He was taught the law of God from his youth up. Even he did not realize—for a time—that his position and condition were desperate before God. Paul puts it like this: *"I was alive once without the law, but when the commandment came, sin revived and I died"* (Rom. 7:9). When he says he was *"alive once,"* he means that he (at that time) thought things were not so bad with him. But when he began to realize what the law really meant, well, then it was different. Then the sin that was already there in his heart was stirred up to become *"exceedingly sinful"* (Rom. 7:13). Thus Paul came to know, by bitter experience, the truth about his own bondage to sin.

But what do we mean when we speak of this law that makes us see our desperate position and condition? Well, there are two ways that we could answer this question, and we find both of them in the Heidelberg Catechism. One way to answer the question would be to say that the law consists of the Ten Commandments, which God gave to Israel on Mount Sinai. (These commandments are found in Ex. 20 and again in Deut. 5.) The other way would be to quote the summary of the law as it was stated by our Lord. (We find this in Matt. 22.) Both of these answers have the same basic meaning. They express the same moral standard in two different and equally valid formulations. But there is a good reason why the Catechism uses the second formulation at this point. It would be wrong to think that God only had one reason for giving us the Ten Commandments. God gave us these laws not only to make us aware of our sin (so that we would seek salvation in Jesus), but also to show us how God wants us to live (as we show our gratitude to him for our salvation). For this reason, the Ten Commandments are expounded later on in the Catechism as the pattern for Christian living. But the main thing that we want to stress here is that there is no difference in the ethical standard held forth in these two formulations. If you kept the Ten Commandments in the right way, you would love God and your neighbor. Similarly, if you loved God and your neighbor in the way you should, you would keep the Ten Commandments.

What God requires, to put it simply, is nothing less than perfection. This is clearly the teaching we find all the way through the Bible. In Leviticus 19:2 we read: *"You shall be holy, for I the LORD your God am holy."* Our Lord Jesus, in his Sermon on the Mount, expressed the same idea when he said, *"Therefore you shall be perfect, just as your Father in heaven is perfect"* (Matt. 5:48). That is why the Catechism asks what it does in Question 5: "Can you keep all this perfectly?" The obvious answer—if we are honest—is that we can't possibly do it. But right now we just want to emphasize that God's standard is perfection and nothing less. Every attempt on the part of sinful men to compromise or to deny this is a hopeless delusion. When we begin to see this, we begin to understand what God intended us to learn through the law. And when we begin to grasp the unpleasant truth about our own position and condition, we also begin to realize our need for Jesus Christ as our only comfort.

QUESTIONS ON THE LESSON

1. Of what two things are many people ignorant?
2. What does God use to dispel our ignorance?

3. If the Ten Commandments and our Lord's summary of the law are the same in substance, why does the Catechism deal with the summary first and the Ten Commandments later?
4. How high is God's ethical standard?

QUESTIONS FOR STUDY AND DISCUSSION

1. Can the Ten Commandments be divided into two parts along the lines of Jesus' first and second commandments? How would you divide them?
2. Does God's standard have to do with our actions or our thoughts?
3. Do you think it is right to speak of men as being in "bondage to sin"? Why?
4. Couldn't someone live according to God's standard if he really tried? What about the rich young man in Mark 10:17–27?

Lord's Day 3

SCRIPTURE READINGS: *Genesis 3:1–5:3;*
Psalm 14; Romans 1:18–32

6. Q. **Did God, then, create man so wicked and perverse?**
    A. By no means; but God created man good, and after His
    own image; that is, in true righteousness and holiness, that
    he might rightly know God his Creator, heartily love Him,
    and live with Him in eternal blessedness to praise and glo-
    rify Him.

7. Q. **Whence, then, comes this depraved nature of man?**
    A. From the fall and disobedience of our first parents, Adam
    and Eve, in Paradise, whereby our nature became so cor-
    rupt that we all are conceived and born in sin.

8. Q. **But are we so corrupt that we are wholly incapable of**
    doing any good, and inclined to all evil?
    A. Yes, indeed; unless we are regenerated by the Spirit of God.

Historical events are very important for the Christian. One of these
events was the creation of man. After God created the universe and
other living creatures, he created man (Gen. 1). After this, there was a
period of time—we are not told how long—during which Adam and
Eve lived on this planet without sinning. During that period of time
there was nothing wrong with man's nature, because it had been created good. It is hard for us to imagine what it was like on this earth
then, because now there is so much evil. But we know that this actually happened, because God tells us so in his Word. After Adam and

Eve were created (Gen. 1:27), the Bible says, "God *saw everything that He had made, and indeed it was very good*" (v. 31).

How, then, did it come about that things today are so different? The answer is well stated by Solomon: "*Truly, this only I have found: that God made man upright, but they have sought out many schemes*" (Eccl. 7:29). It all started with another event that is recorded in the Bible. It was the temptation of Eve and Adam and their subjection of themselves to Satan. The account of this is found in Genesis 3, and it is also something that actually happened. In other words, this story is not—as some falsely say today—just a myth or a symbol. Yes, there are even some theologians who say that the word *Adam* does not refer to a certain, particular man who lived on the earth in early history. No, they say, the story of Adam is simply the story of every man. As you read the story, you simply say to yourself, "Yes, that describes my own experience as a person." The only real Adam, they say, is just what is common to the experience of all men.

Now there is an element of truth in this. We are like Adam—all of us are. But why are we like Adam? Can a myth or a symbol help us with that question? No, of course not. But we do have an answer to it when we take the biblical record to be true. If Adam and Eve really were perfect to begin with and then disobeyed God (as Gen. 3 says they did), and if we are their descendants, then there is no great difficulty in understanding why we are like them and basically like one another. Just as an apple tree has many apples—and all of them are Delicious apples if the tree is a Delicious apple tree—so it is with the human race because of the first sin of Adam and Eve. Because of our relationship with our first parents, we share their fallen nature.

So the result of the historical fall of Adam and Eve is that our nature is what can well be described as "poisoned" and "corrupt from conception." In Reformed theology, this is usually called the doctrine of total depravity. To understand this concept we must clearly grasp two things. First, the word *depravity* indicates that human nature has been damaged. If you could place man as he is now alongside man as he was at creation, it would be like comparing a rotten apple with a good one. Second, the word *total* indicates the extent of the depravity. But here we have to be careful, because we do not mean that the ruin of man is so complete that there is nothing left that is human—nothing left to remind us that man was made in God's image. No, just as the whole ancient city of Athens now lies in ruins, and yet those ruins still have a certain grandeur that reminds us of the city's former beauty and glory, so it is with the nature of fallen man. The word *total* simply means that there is no part of man's nature as it now is—fallen in Adam—that did not suffer corruption. The whole man—body and soul; mind, heart, and will—has been fatally damaged. That is why the Bible says there is no hope for man at all unless God makes him a new creature.

It is for this reason that the Bible uses very strong words when it speaks of the remedy needed for our fallen condition. Jesus said, *"You must be born again"* (John 3:7). Paul had the same thing in mind when he said that God *"made us alive together with Christ"* and *"raised us up together"* with him (Eph. 2:5–6). John, in the last book of the Bible, calls the same thing *"the first resurrection"* (Rev. 20:5; cf. John 5:25). The Bible uses such strong words because it wants us to be very clear about one thing: there is nothing in fallen men themselves, by nature, that can bring about the change that is needed. If a man is to be saved, it will have to be by God's almighty power and unmerited mercy, and that only. But of that we will learn more as we continue our studies of the Heidelberg Catechism.

QUESTIONS ON THE LESSON

1. Has the human race always been characterized by violence?
2. What caused such a change in human nature?
3. Why are the descendants of Adam and Eve also corrupt?
4. Is there anything left of the former goodness of man?
5. Why do men need to be "born again," or, to use another figure of speech, "raised up from death"?

QUESTIONS FOR STUDY AND DISCUSSION

1. If the human race has evolved, how does the biblical story of the first sin of Adam and Eve fit in?
2. Are little children sinful too? What about infants in the womb?
3. In theology we speak of men as being totally corrupt. Are men as bad as they could be or could things get even worse? How bad could they get?
4. Over the entrance to the United Nations building in New York there

is the inscription, "They shall beat their swords into plowshares, and their spears into pruninghooks: nation shall not lift up a sword against nation, neither shall they learn war any more." This is taken from Micah 4:3. Do you think this goal is achievable in view of what we have learned in this lesson? Why or why not?

LORD'S DAY 4

SCRIPTURE READINGS: *Psalm 103:1–18;*
Exodus 32:1–34:17; Nahum 1:1–8

9. **Q. Does not God, then, wrong man by requiring of him in
    His law that which he cannot perform?**

    A. Not at all; for God made man capable of performing it; but
    man, through the instigation of the devil, by his own wil-
    ful disobedience, deprived himself and all his posterity of
    these gifts.

10. **Q. Will God suffer such disobedience and apostasy to go
    unpunished?**

    A. By no means; but He is terribly displeased with our origi-
    nal as well as actual sins; and will punish them by a just
    judgment temporally and eternally, as He has declared,
    *Cursed is every one who continueth not in all things that are
    written in the book of the law, to do them.*

11. **Q. Is, then, God not also merciful?**

    A. God is indeed merciful, but He is also just; therefore His
    justice requires that sin which is committed against the
    most high majesty of God, be also punished with extreme,
    that is, with everlasting punishment of body and soul.

In the previous section of the Catechism, we learned that we are not
able to keep God's commandments—and that God requires us to be
perfect. This, of course, makes us all want to say: "It isn't fair! It isn't
fair for God to demand perfection when we lack the ability to comply

21

with that demand." Suppose, for instance, that God punished a fish for not walking—or a cow for not flying! Is it not self-evident that this would be unjust? It surely is not fair, or just, to punish a creature for not doing what it was never given the ability to do. So why can't we say the same thing about man, since he is not able to keep God's commandments perfectly? The answer is very simple: when God created man, he was able to keep God's commandments. It is entirely man's own fault that he is no longer able to do what he was able to do in the beginning.

Let us try to illustrate this with an analogy. A certain father was very wealthy. He therefore decided to give to each of his children a large inheritance that included a beautiful mansion and a large bank account earning enough interest for the child to live without any worries. Would it be wrong if that father expected each child to take good care of the inheritance given to him? Suppose that one son used all his money to gamble on the horses and then sold his house because he fell so deeply in debt. Would it be unfair if his father then said, "Don't ask me for any more money! I gave you all you could ever need, and it is entirely your own fault that you are now destitute"? No, of course it would not be unfair. And neither is it unfair when God maintains his requirements for us. That is why the Bible says what it does about breaking even one of God's commandments. We are under God's just judgment if we do not do everything he has commanded (Deut. 27:26). What we must remember, then, is that originally man was able to do what God required. It is only because the human race squandered its God-given inheritance that this is no longer true. So God is perfectly just when he refuses to excuse us.

To us this may seem harsh. Right away we may begin to ask, "But isn't God also a God of mercy?" The answer—found many times in the Bible—is, "Yes, indeed, God is merciful" (e.g., Ex. 34:6–7; Ps. 103:8–9). But there is one thing that God will never do because of his mercy. He will never compromise his justice. He will never say, "I guess I will just let it go—this great sin that man has committed." No, God's justice is just as great (and unchangeable) as his mercy. He cannot deny himself (2 Tim. 2:13). His sense of justice must be satisfied no less than his sense of mercy. And this means that payment must be made for the sins that we have committed, and that payment must be the infinite punishment demanded for perfect justice. It was, after all, an infinite God that man sinned against—and *infinite* means "without measure or limit." So the punishment that is just and fair must also be "without measure." And that means, for those who are lost, punishment that is eternal. Of this we will learn more in a later section of this study. But before we come to that, we must first consider God's merciful provision for the salvation of those who repent of their sin and come to believe in the Lord Jesus.

QUESTIONS ON THE LESSON

1. Why is it "fair" for God to demand of man what man is not able to perform?
2. Why has the theory of evolution made it more difficult for many to accept the teaching of this section of the Catechism?
3. If God is merciful, why must the full penalty for sin nevertheless be paid?

QUESTIONS FOR STUDY AND DISCUSSION

1. Do you think it is fair that God regards us as enemies (right from conception—see Ps. 51:5; Rom. 5:8–10) because of Adam's sin? Can you think of similar examples in life, in which a person is regarded as an enemy because of the actions of another person?
2. Do you think that God should let Hitler into heaven? Why or why not? Should he let any criminals into heaven? Should he let you into heaven? Wouldn't the presence of any sin in heaven ruin it?
3. If God were to let one person "off the hook" or to allow one sin to remain unjudged, he would be an unjust judge. What would you think of a high court judge who let someone off just because he liked him or was related to him? Would God do such a thing?

PART II

❖

DELIVERANCE

LORD'S DAY 5

SCRIPTURE READINGS: *Leviticus 4;*
Matthew 25; Hebrews 10

12. **Q. Since, then, by the righteous judgment of God we deserve temporal and eternal punishment, is there no way by which we may escape that punishment and be again received into favor?**

    A. God will have His justice satisfied; therefore we must make full satisfaction to the same, either by ourselves, or by another.

13. **Q. But can we ourselves make this satisfaction?**

    A. By no means; on the contrary, we daily increase our debt.

14. **Q. Can there be found anywhere a mere creature able to satisfy for us?**

    A. None; for, first, God will not punish any other creature for the sin which man has committed; and, further, no mere creature can sustain the burden of God's eternal wrath against sin, and deliver others from it.

15. **Q. What manner of mediator and deliverer, then, must we seek?**

    A. One who is a true and righteous man, and yet more powerful than all creatures; that is, one who is withal true God.

We all, by nature, prefer to think of God only in terms of his goodness and mercy. We would like him to be the kind of God who is willing just to let our sins go, without insisting on justice. As a matter of fact, that is

27

the way many people today do think about God. But they are only deceiving themselves. When they do this, they are really imagining a false
god—an idol. For in truth God is holy and righteous and will not compromise justice. He says, *"I will not justify the wicked"* (Ex. 23:7). As the
apostle John reminds us, *"God is light"* and *"in Him is no darkness at all"*
(1 John 1:5). Light is the natural symbol of God's absolute justice and
truth, just as darkness is the symbol of Satan's kingdom of error and evil.
Because God is light, it is very foolish to think for even one moment that
he will go easy on sin. The truth is that not one single sin—not even one
we might call "a very little one"—will be remitted without full payment.

Two things in God's holy Word allow no other conclusion. First,
Scripture plainly tells us that some men will be eternally punished. We
emphasize this, not because we like to say it, but because we cannot
deny it, if we believe the Lord Jesus. It was he, more than any other,
who plainly spoke of this awesome reality. (As you read through the
gospel of Matthew, you will be amazed how often Jesus speaks of eternal damnation. Read Matt. 25, for instance.)

A second thing that makes it abundantly clear that God will punish every sin in full is the suffering and death of Jesus. Even though Jesus himself was entirely free of all sin and guilt, he still had to die in
order to redeem his people. If it had been at all possible for God just to
let sin go, then surely he would have done so in order to spare Jesus
such terrible suffering. But the Bible says that God *"did not spare His
own Son"* (Rom. 8:32). If even the sins of believers had to be punished
in Jesus, then it is a vain thing to imagine that unbelievers will escape.

It follows, then—since we are sinners—that we are left with only
two options. Either we will have to satisfy God's justice ourselves or
someone else will have to do it for us. There is no third possibility. And
if anything is clear in the Bible—from Genesis to Revelation—it is that
there is no way that we can ever satisfy God's absolute justice for ourselves. That is why there is eternal punishment. It goes on and on forever for one simple reason: there is no way that a sinner can ever finish making an adequate payment for sin. Suppose, for example, that you
owed an infinite sum of money—so much money that even the fastest
computer could never add it all up. Suppose, too, that you repaid that
money at the rate of one thousand dollars a day for one million years.
Do you realize that you would still be at the beginning of repayment?
The reason is that an infinite sum of money can never be repaid by any
number of finite payments. It is like that with our debt to God. We have

sinned against an infinite God, and there is no way that we can fully repay him by suffering as finite creatures.

But suppose a man had an ox or a lamb, and he made that ox or lamb suffer in his place. Would that satisfy the justice of God? Would that be enough to "even the scales of justice"? Again, the answer is no! In spite of the fact that God himself at one time commanded animal sacrifices, these were never enough to pay for a man's sins. The Scripture says, *"It is not possible that the blood of bulls and goats could take away sins"* (Heb. 10:4). The reason is quite simple: animals are not equal to man in nature and value. Animals were not made in the image of God, and they do not have a moral nature. For the same reason, even the angels could not redeem man, for they are not made in God's image and are therefore not man's equal. That is why the Bible says our redeemer had to be truly human.

> *"Inasmuch then as the children have partaken of flesh and blood, He Himself likewise shared in the same, that through death He might destroy him who had the power of death, that is, the devil, and release those who through fear of death were all their lifetime subject to bondage. For indeed He does not give aid to angels, but He does give aid to the seed of Abraham. Therefore, in all things He had to be made like His brethren, that He might be a merciful and faithful High Priest in things pertaining to God, to make propitiation for the sins of the people."* (Heb. 2:14–17)

One could imagine one righteous man dying to redeem one other person (if such a righteous man could be found, and he were willing to do it). But even if such a person could be found, he could not redeem many people—unless he were not only a man but also an infinite person. And there is no one who is infinite except God. Thus, we need a Savior who is both divine and human. There is one, and only one, who meets these requirements. It is the Lord Jesus, who is revealed to us in the Bible as the divine-human Savior. We will see this clearly as we continue in the next section of the Catechism.

QUESTIONS ON THE LESSON

1. In what way do many people imagine a false god?
2. What two facts in Scripture make it certain that not even one "small" sin will go unpunished?

3. In Scripture, who speaks about eternal damnation the most?
4. Why could not an angel have become man to die for our sins (as the Jehovah's Witnesses say), instead of the very Son of God?
5. Why could not some man other than Jesus die for our sins?

Questions for Study and Discussion

1. Do many Christians falsely think of God as being only full of love and not justice? Why do they, when the Bible is so plain on the subject?
2. Is it fair that a gossip and a murderer should both be punished with eternal damnation? Isn't murder much worse than gossip?
3. What about your sinful thoughts? Will God let you "off the hook" as long as you don't put them into action?

LORD'S DAY 6

SCRIPTURE READINGS: *Psalm 110; Isaiah 53*

16. Q. **Why must He be a true and righteous man?**

    A. Because the justice of God requires that the same human nature which has sinned should make satisfaction for sin, and because one who himself is a sinner cannot satisfy for others.

17. Q. **Why must He withal be true God?**

    A. That by the power of His Godhead He might bear in His human nature the burden of God's wrath; and that He might obtain for us, and restore to us, righteousness and life.

18. Q. **But who is that Mediator who is at once true God and a true, righteous man?**

    A. Our Lord Jesus Christ, *who was made unto us wisdom from God, and righteousness and sanctification, and redemption.*

19. Q. **Whence do you know this?**

    A. From the holy gospel, which God Himself first revealed in Paradise; afterwards published by the holy patriarchs and prophets, and foreshadowed by the sacrifices and other ceremonies of the law; and lastly fulfilled by His only begotten Son.

We saw in the previous section that the only Savior who can provide what we need is one who is both human and divine. In this section,

this great truth is spelled out even more fully. In addition, something
else is made clear that is very important. It is the fact that this doctrine
of Christ—as one person who has two natures—is really the central
teaching of both the Old and the New Testament Scriptures.

Let us begin at the beginning (the book of Gen.). After the Serpent tempted Adam and Eve and they succumbed to the temptation,
God spoke these prophetic words to the Serpent (because the Serpent
did not act on its own but was the instrument of Satan, these words
were also addressed to Satan through the Serpent): *"And I will put en-
mity between you and the woman, and between your seed and her Seed; He
shall bruise your head, and you shall bruise His heel"* (Gen. 3:15). Obviously, this statement did not tell our first parents everything they may
have wished to know. But it did tell them the main thing they needed
to know. For one thing, it told them that God himself would put en-
mity between the seed of the Serpent and the seed of the woman. It
was also quite clear that the *"seed"* that God had in mind would be one
person—a male person—who would be mighty enough to inflict a
greater wound on Satan than Satan could inflict on him. This clearly
suggested a Savior who would be both human (as the descendant of the
woman) and yet more than human (in order to be stronger than Satan). Clearly, there would be a single person who combined these qualities, a single person who would destroy the works of the Devil.

This same basic concept is gradually unfolded, more and more fully,
throughout the rest of the Old Testament. You see it, for instance, in
the psalms of David, whom God made king over his covenant people.
This is what God promised David: *"When your days are fulfilled and you
rest with your fathers, I will set up your seed after you, who will come from
your body, and I will establish his kingdom. He shall build a house for My
name, and I will establish the throne of his kingdom forever"* (2 Sam.
7:12–13). In some of the psalms, David speaks about this great promise
that God made to him. In Psalm 110, for example, David writes, *"The
LORD said to my Lord, 'Sit at My right hand, till I make Your enemies Your
footstool'"* (v. 1). In this statement, David expresses what God had
promised to the illustrious descendant who was to rule in the future.
The interesting thing is that in this statement David calls his own son
(or, according to the Hebrew idiom, his own descendant) "Lord"! Now,
to say the least, this is highly unusual. Ordinarily an ancestor is given
honor by the descendant. Why, then, does David give honor to his descendant as Lord? This was the very question that Jesus put to the Jews.

After quoting this passage, Jesus went on to ask, *"If David then calls Him 'Lord,' how is He his Son?"* (Matt. 22:45). The answer, of course, is that Jesus is a descendant of David as to his human nature. But, at the same time, he is superior to David because he is also divine. We see that already in the Old Testament these two elements stood together: there was to be one great Savior, or Messiah, but he was to be both divine and human. Sometimes the Old Testament writers spoke of him in such a way as to emphasize that he would be human. At other times his divine nature was emphasized. But a constant line of teaching through the whole Old Testament consistently shows that there was to be one great Savior, who would be both human and divine.

Right after the fall of man, it was evidently God himself who made the first sacrifice for sinners. This is implied in Genesis 3:21, which says, *"Also for Adam and his wife the LORD God made tunics of skin, and clothed them."* From that time on, godly people always approached God through animal sacrifices. In Genesis 4, for example, we read about Cain and Abel, the sons of Adam. God *"respected Abel and his offering, but He did not respect Cain and his offering"* (vv. 4–5). There was good reason for this, for, as the Scripture says, *"By faith Abel offered to God a more excellent sacrifice than Cain"* (Heb. 11:4). It was more excellent because Abel sacrificed a living creature—a sinless creature—offering it up in death by the shedding of blood. This was important, because *"without shedding of blood there is no remission [i.e., forgiveness]"* (Heb. 9:22). The fact that God rejected Cain's bloodless offering and accepted Abel's blood sacrifice proved that no one could be saved without a dying substitute.

In the rest of the Old Testament we see a deepening of this concept. In the law of Moses, for instance—which came later on—there is a whole series of detailed requirements for the sacrifices that God would accept from his people. But why were there so many? Perhaps there were several reasons. But the main reason was to make it clear that the cost of paying for sin is high. In fact, it was so high that even great quantities of blood—animal blood—did not suffice. That is why the inspired prophet Isaiah finally wrote of the coming Messiah in terms that remind us of these animal sacrifices (Isa. 53). In this way God made it clear that the real—the final—atonement for sin would be made by the seed of the woman!

> *"Surely He has borne our griefs and carried our sorrows; yet we esteemed Him stricken, smitten by God, and afflicted. But He was wounded for our transgressions, He was bruised for our iniquities;*

the chastisement for our peace was upon Him, and by His stripes we are healed . . . it pleased the LORD to bruise Him; He has put Him to grief. When You make His soul an offering for sin, He shall see His seed, He shall prolong His days, and the pleasure of the LORD shall prosper in His hand." (Isa. 53:4–5, 10)

It was already clear in the Old Testament that animal sacrifices, in themselves, were not enough to atone for man's sin. There had to be something better. There had to be the sacrifice of a divine-human Savior. The New Testament shows how God fulfilled his great promise by sending such a redeemer. When the perfect and final sacrifice was finally made in the person and work of Jesus Christ, then at last God's people could really be free—put right with God forever. For, as God himself has told us, *"we have been sanctified through the offering of the body of Jesus Christ once for all."* Yes, *"for by one offering He has perfected forever those who are being sanctified"* (Heb. 10:10, 14).

QUESTIONS ON THE LESSON

1. What basic things did Genesis 3:15 tell our first parents?
2. What does 2 Samuel 7:12–13 prove with respect to the person of Christ?
3. Why did Jesus quote Psalm 110:1 in his exchange with the Jews?
4. Why was Cain's offering rejected while Abel's was accepted?
5. What important fact was made self-evident by the vast number of animal sacrifices under the Old Testament?
6. Why does Isaiah use the terminology of the sacrificial lamb when speaking of the suffering of the Messiah?

QUESTIONS FOR STUDY AND DISCUSSION

1. Answer 16 of the Catechism says that a sinner cannot pay for the sin of others. Why not?
2. Using a good Bible dictionary, study the various sacrifices commanded by God in the Old Testament. Try to learn the purpose of each kind of sacrifice.
3. What does the sacrificial system teach us about the work of Christ?

4. What works of the Devil must be destroyed? Christ came to destroy the works of the Devil. Why then are the Devil's works still around today?

Lord's Day 7

SCRIPTURE READINGS: *Hebrews 11;*
Acts 16:11–15; Ephesians 2:1–10

20. Q. **Are all men, then, saved by Christ as they perished through Adam?**
     A. No; but only those who by a true faith are ingrafted into Him and receive all His benefits.

21. Q. **What is true faith?**
     A. True faith is not only a sure knowledge, whereby I hold for truth all that God has revealed to us in His Word, but also a firm confidence which the Holy Spirit works in my heart by the gospel, that not only to others, but to me also, remission of sins, everlasting righteousness and salvation are freely given by God, merely of grace, only for the sake of Christ's merits.

22. Q. **What, then, is necessary for a Christian to believe?**
     A. All that is promised us in the gospel, which the articles of our catholic and undoubted Christian faith teach us in a summary.

23. Q. **What are these articles?**
     A.   I. *I believe in God the Father, Almighty, Maker of heaven and earth.*
         II. *And in Jesus Christ, His only begotten Son, our Lord;*
        III. *Who was conceived by the Holy Spirit, born of the virgin Mary;*

    IV. *Suffered under Pontius Pilate; was crucified, dead, and buried; He descended into hell;*

    V. *The third day He rose again from the dead;*

    VI. *He ascended into heaven, and sitteth at the right hand of God the Father Almighty;*

    VII. *From thence He shall come to judge the living and the dead.*

    VIII. *I believe in the Holy Spirit.*

    IX. *I believe in a holy catholic Church, the communion of saints;*

    X. *The forgiveness of sins;*

    XI. *The resurrection of the body;*

    XII. *And the life everlasting.*

When a person says, "I just somehow have faith that everything will turn out right," it is not really faith that this person has—it is hope. The person hopes that all will be well. Again, people sometimes use the word *faith* when they should use the word *want.* "If you believe a thing strongly enough," it is said, "then it will surely happen." What this really means is that one's wish or desire is so strong that somehow external reality will conform with it. On this view, faith is something that comes out of a man and imposes itself on the external world. On this view we could say, "Faith is the cause of things hoped for, the producer of things as yet unseen." But such is not true faith.

    True faith is something entirely different. It is different, in the first place, because it comes to me from the outside. You see, in actual fact there is only one reality. It is not what I may imagine it to be, but what God has actually made it to be. So what I need in order to have true faith is reliable information about this reality. And this is exactly what God has given me in his holy Word. In his Word, the Bible, I learn about creation, the fall of man, and the whole plan of salvation. It is when this information is properly received by me that I begin to have faith. Thus the Bible defines faith in exactly the opposite way from the false definition so common today. "*Now faith is the substance of things hoped for, the evidence of things not seen*" (Heb. 11:1). It is produced in me, in other words, by the input that comes to me through God's revelation in the Bible. Take the creation of the world, for example. "*By faith we understand that the worlds were framed by the word of God, so that the things which are seen were not made of things which are visible*" (Heb.

11:3). So God tells me in his Word, the Bible, the factual data about creation. I do not project this out of my own imagination. No, God injects it into me by his revelation. The true data of reality form the conviction within me. It is for this reason that the apostle says, "*So then faith comes by hearing, and hearing by the word of God*" (Rom. 10:17).

We might illustrate this in a simple way by thinking of a little child and his mother. Why is it that this little child trusts his mother, but is so shy around other people? Is it because of something the child has done to produce trustworthiness in the mother? Or is it because of what the mother has done? Obviously, it is because of what the mother has done. She has taken care of her child since he was born, and the child knows, and is persuaded, that she can be relied on. It is precisely the lack of comparable data with respect to others that makes the child shy when he comes to them. The child's faith is something produced from the outside—and so it is with Christian faith. As a matter of fact, it is only Christianity that provides a source for true faith, because there is only one reality and that reality is what God has revealed in the Bible.

The question will therefore arise: "Why, then, do some men believe when they hear the message of the Bible, while others do not?" The answer is that two things are essential for faith. The first thing is God's revelation to us in the Bible. We have already seen why this is so. The other essential thing is a capacity in us to receive this revelation. But this capacity is not present in us by nature. That is why Jesus said, "*Unless one is born again, he cannot see . . . [or] enter the kingdom of God*" (John 3:3, 5). This is so because "*the natural man does not receive the things of the Spirit of God, for they are foolishness to him; nor can he know them, because they are spiritually discerned*" (1 Cor. 2:14). It is for this reason that the Bible says we must be "*made . . . alive*" by the power of the Holy Spirit (Eph. 2:5). When the Spirit of God does this work (which is commonly called "regeneration"), a man will be willing to receive the truth of divine revelation (Phil. 2:13).

What happens within the heart when a man is "born again" is comparable to what happened visibly in some of the miracles of Christ. He caused the blind to see and the dead to come to life. When a blind man's sight was restored, he could see again. When a dead man was raised up from the dead, he could move again. And so it is that the man who is born again (or regenerated) by the power of the Holy Spirit can understand—and be convinced by—the content of the biblical message. So, from the outside comes the information (or data) that produces faith in a man who is able to receive it. And it is the Holy Spirit who changes man on the inside so that he has the capacity to receive that information in a saving manner.

The first thing you have, then, when the light of God's truth is received by a regenerate man, is knowledge. A person at last begins to understand the real universe in which he is living. He begins to see himself as a creature, in a created and meaningful universe, having a great destiny, and so on. He comes to realize that man fell, but also that Jesus came to die for sinners. When true knowledge of these things (as well as other things) is formed in the mind of that man, it cannot fail to lead to conviction. A man who understands these things cannot fail to see the importance of them. He will realize his own need of salvation. So knowledge, in the regenerate man, always leads to conviction. And this, finally, brings one to trust in the Lord Jesus for eternal salvation. True faith—saving faith—always includes knowledge, conviction, and trust.

One question that is often asked is, How much do I need to know—and believe—in order to be saved? The answer, in principle, is this: I must believe "all that God has revealed to us in his Word." If God tells us anything clearly in his Word, then—if we have true faith—we will receive it. We will not reject it in order to place our confidence in our own mind or reason instead of the Bible. The thief on the cross near Jesus did not have time to learn very much. But he did believe everything the Lord Jesus told him. And so it must be with all true believers. However, the most basic things are summarized in the earliest creed of the Christian church, the Apostles' Creed. It is the content of this creed that we will be considering in the next several sections of our study.

QUESTIONS ON THE LESSON

1. What are some of the things that people call faith that are not really faith in the biblical sense?
2. What is the ultimate source of a man's faith, if it is true faith?
3. Why do some believe when they hear the message of the Bible, while others do not?
4. How much of the Bible does a person need to believe in order to be saved?

QUESTIONS FOR STUDY AND DISCUSSION

1. Since we must have reliable information about the world, ourselves, and God in order to have true faith, it is essential to know that the Bible is reliable. Why can we be confident that the Bible is reliable?

2. Suppose there is a person who believes in God, acknowledges his own sinfulness, and accepts that the Bible is the Word of God. He believes much of what the Bible teaches, but he just can't accept the idea of the resurrection from the dead. That sounds too much like a fairy tale to him, and it is too crassly materialistic for his way of thinking. Does this one difficulty mean that he does not have true faith (cf. 1 Cor. 15:12–19)?

3. Discuss the common view that a person believes on Christ and then is born again (regenerated) as a result of his faith. What is the source of faith according to this view? What is the nature of faith according to this view? How does the teaching of Ephesians 2:1–10 contradict this view?

LORD'S DAY 8

SCRIPTURE READINGS: *Hebrews 1:1–4;*
John 1:1–18; Genesis 18; Matthew 28:18–20

24. **Q. How are these articles divided?**
A. Into three parts: the first is of God the Father and our creation; the second of God the Son and our redemption; the
third of God the Holy Spirit and our sanctification.

25. **Q. Since there is but one divine Being, why do you speak**
of three, Father, Son, and Holy Spirit?
A. Because God has so revealed Himself in His Word that
these three distinct persons are the one, true, and eternal
God.

Among the various religions of the world, one is unique. The Christian
religion is unique because it has a doctrine of God that sets it quite
apart. This doctrine can be stated in three simple propositions: (1) There
is only one true God; (2) the true God exists in three persons; and (3)
each of the three persons is distinct from the other two.

We know that this is so because God has revealed it to us. In the
Bible, the true God has gradually made himself known to us as the Father, the Son, and the Holy Spirit. We say "gradually" because God did
not suddenly grant the whole content of this revelation to us. No, it
was given over a long period of time. The Bible puts it like this: "*God,
who at various times and in different ways spoke in time past to the fathers
by the prophets, has in these last days spoken to us by His Son*" (Heb. 1:1–2).

You notice, from this statement, first, that God's self-revelation was
less direct at the beginning. Then, later on, he himself came in the per-

son of Jesus Christ. It is no wonder, then, that in the Old Testament, emphasis is placed on the fact that there is but one true God. *"Hear, O Israel,"* cried Moses, as God's inspired prophet, *"the* LORD *our God, the* LORD *is one"* (Deut. 6:4). It was only later on—after the rejection of polytheism (the teaching that there are many gods)—that God revealed himself as multipersonal. As a matter of fact, it was not clearly and fully revealed until the coming of Jesus Christ and (a little later on) the pouring out of the Holy Spirit. This does not mean that there is nothing in the Old Testament that suggests that God is triune (one God in three persons). As a matter of fact, there is much in the Old Testament that can only be understood in the light of the fact that God is triune. Take, for instance, some of the passages in which we read about the angel of the Lord (such as Gen. 18). Now in some sense this angel of the Lord was distinct from God in heaven. Yet, at the same time, this angel himself is called Lord!

A second thing that we learn from this statement in the book of Hebrews is that God's revelation came to completion in the person and work of Jesus Christ. That is why the apostles so clearly taught that there are three persons in the Godhead. There was no way they could avoid this truth, after they had been with Jesus and had seen the outpouring of the Spirit. They knew, for instance, from the prayer life of Jesus, that there is a heavenly Father distinct from Jesus the Son. Yet they also knew, from the claims of Christ (and from the mighty works he did, fully proving the claims), that he himself was God. Then, after Jesus went back to be with the Father, they (both Father and Son) sent the Holy Spirit. And the fact that the Holy Spirit could come to be with them while Jesus himself had gone away from them showed that the Spirit was also a distinct person. From data such as this, the apostles were left with no option but to believe in one true God, and yet to understand that he exists in three divine persons.

When we understand that the one true God does indeed exist in three persons, we can see that each of these persons is distinct from the other two. It is clear, for instance, that only Jesus (the second person of the divine Trinity) took upon himself our human nature. Only he died to make atonement for our sins. It was not the Father who died, nor was it the Holy Spirit. Again, it is perfectly clear that Christ was sent by the Father, not by the Holy Spirit. The Holy Spirit, however, was himself sent by the Lord Jesus Christ and the Father. Again, it is the Holy Spirit alone who is said in the Bible to regenerate God's people, so that they can know and believe. It is little wonder, then, that the oldest creed of the Christian church is a triune confession, setting forth faith in the one true God who exists in three persons.

To sum it up, let us think of the words of the apostle John. They make it clear that we must believe in each of these persons. *"Whoever denies the Son does not have the Father either; he who acknowledges the Son has the Father also"* (1 John 2:23). Those who do not know—and believe in—this triune God do not have God but only an idol. So let us make sure that we confess this true God with the church of all ages.

QUESTIONS ON THE LESSON

1. Who are the three persons of the Godhead?
2. Cite some evidences of the triune nature of God that are found in the Old Testament.
3. Mention two or three ways in which God has revealed his triune nature to us.
4. If we do not worship and serve the triune God, what do we worship and serve?

QUESTIONS FOR STUDY AND DISCUSSION

1. What response would you give to the Jehovah's Witnesses, who claim that the doctrine of the Trinity is obviously false since it is a contradiction to speak of three being one?
2. Discuss the reason for the Jews' attempt to kill Jesus in John 5:18 and John 10:30–33.
3. Discuss the philosophical problem of the one and the many in view of the doctrine of the Trinity.

LORD'S DAY 9

SCRIPTURE READINGS: *Matthew 14:15–21;*
John 2:1–11; 2 Peter 3:1–13

26. Q. **What do you believe when you say:** *I believe in God the*
     Father, Almighty, Maker of heaven and earth?
     A. That the eternal Father of our Lord Jesus Christ, who of
     nothing made heaven and earth with all that is in them,
     who likewise upholds and governs the same by His eternal
     counsel and providence, is for the sake of Christ His Son
     my God and my Father; in whom I so trust as to have no
     doubt that He will provide me with all things necessary
     for body and soul; and further, that whatever evil He sends
     upon me in this vale of tears, He will turn to my good; for
     He is able to do it, being almighty God, and willing also,
     being a faithful Father.

When the Heidelberg Catechism was written, the doctrine of creation
was not so much argued as assumed. This is no longer true. Today there
are even many Christians who seem to want to minimize the greatness
of God with respect to creation. This is undoubtedly due to the tremendous influence of the false theory of evolution. The basic ingredients of
this theory can be briefly stated. The material universe is seen as something eternal, and as constantly changing. Vast amounts of time—plus
chance—supposedly produced the present form of our universe.

It would be hard to think of anything more completely contrary
to the Bible. Yet the strange thing is that many Christians today try to
blend the two—creation and evolution—in what is called theistic evolution. In this way it is supposed that a Christian can believe in God

44

and yet—at the same time—go along with the scientific community of this age as it describes a supposed process of evolution that took millions and even billions of years.

One of the main arguments used by those who take this compromise position is that the universe appears to be very old. They assert that God would be misleading us if he made things to have the appearance of age when—as a matter of fact—they were not old at all. Our answer is that this is a false charge. God does not mislead anyone when he makes things having the appearance of age. What he does is to manifest his power. Do we not see this very clearly from some of the biblical miracles? It will be sufficient, here, to mention three particular miracles: the miraculous supply of oil (2 Kings 4:1–7), the changing of water into wine (John 2:1–11), and the feeding of the five thousand (Matt. 14:15–21). In each of these miracles God put forth his creative power. And in each case something instantly came into existence having the appearance of age. For example, the wine at the wedding feast seemed, to those who drank it, to be the oldest and therefore the best wine. In truth it was old wine with respect to its qualities. Yet we know that Christ had created it only moments before they drank it. Did our Lord, then, mislead people? No, of course not. He simply manifested his divine power.

It is certainly clear, from the data of Scripture, that man did not have an evolutionary background. We know this from such things as these: (1) Genesis not only says that God made Adam from the dust of the earth (2:7). It also says that when man dies, he returns to the dust again (3:19). The inspired writer, Moses, evidently saw these two as parallel. Since man does not return to any prehuman form at death, it is clear that Moses did not intend for us to understand that we came from such, either. (2) We also know that *"Adam was formed first, then Eve"* (1 Tim. 2:13). There is no way that such a thing could possibly have happened through any evolutionary process of reproduction. For the male and the female of any species to come into existence at different times is out of the question. The only way that such a thing could have happened was by God creating them directly. Some are therefore willing to admit that God did create man—on the spot, so to speak—adult in appearance. And yet they stumble over what they call "the problem" of an appearance of age in the rest of creation. (3) In Paul's greatest New Testament letter, there is a passage of profound importance (Rom. 5:12–21). If there really was one man created by God at the beginning of history, then we can understand in some small degree how we got where we are now. We can understand why men are all sinners. But that is not all. We also see that God can create a new humanity through the saving work of Jesus Christ.

There is an interrelationship between the doctrines of the Bible. They constitute a system. It is only when we receive—and believe—the system of doctrine taught in the Bible that we experience the comfort and assurance that we need. On the one hand, we see that God is merciful and compassionate to us when we are in fellowship with Christ. But we also see, on the other hand, that our comfort is not grounded in God's compassion alone; it is also grounded in the fact that he is the almighty God who created all things. Because he created all things, it is not difficult for him to rule over them. Even the things that stagger our imagination are not beyond him. Take, for instance, the problem of death. A man dies. We bury his physical body in the grave. We do what we can to preserve that body (with good biblical precedent). But we know that it will (let us be literal) rot away and decay. How then can we possibly believe that that very body will yet be raised up again at the Last Day? The answer is—the answer can only be—that we have no idea how it can happen. But we do know that it will happen. We do not find it hard to believe when we think about the truth of creation! Here, before our very eyes, is the awesome universe—and God created it. He spoke and it appeared. In six days he then brought it to perfection. So why should I doubt that he can resurrect my corrupted body?

The doctrine of creation *ex nihilo* (out of nothing) is an essential Christian teaching. Even if we had no revelation of God in the Bible—and in the historical person of Jesus Christ—we would still be *"without excuse"* if we did not believe it (Rom. 1:20). But we do have the Bible and we do have God's self-manifestation in Jesus Christ. Our Lord did many mighty works. He showed that he could speak and "there it was." He could command and things came into existence. It is our conviction, therefore, that the miracles of Jesus Christ are exhibit A when it comes to the doctrine of creation. We must never allow our thinking to move in the direction of minimizing God's awesome power.

Science can only deal with things that already exist. It does not have any special power to see behind the things that exist in order to tell us how they came to be. No, at this point we must simply believe. (The evolutionist "believes" just as truly as the Christian. But he chooses to believe in what is created rather than in the Creator.) For *"by faith we understand that the worlds were framed by the word of God, so that the things which are seen were not made of things which are visible"* (Heb. 11:3). May God grant that we may believe and not compromise his glory and honor.

QUESTIONS ON THE LESSON

1. What do the miracles recorded in the Bible tell us about creation?
2. What biblical data show us that Adam had no ancestors?
3. How is the doctrine of creation related to the doctrine of the resurrection?
4. Is it the Christian or the evolutionist who takes things on faith?

QUESTIONS FOR STUDY AND DISCUSSION

1. Can time plus chance produce anything? If you found a carefully crafted and intricately designed timepiece in a remote desert, would you be inclined to think that it was produced by the operation of the wind upon the sand over long ages? Why are some people inclined to think the universe just happened?
2. Consider the marvels of the universe—its vastness, its design, its complexity and intricacy. How great is God?

Lord's Day 10

SCRIPTURE READINGS: *Deuteronomy 28;*
Genesis 37; 39–46; 50:15–21; Romans 8:28

27.   Q. **What do you mean by the providence of God?**

      A. The almighty and everywhere present power of God, whereby, as it were by His hand, He still upholds heaven, earth, and all creatures, and so governs them that herbs and grass, rain and drought, fruitful and barren years, food and drink, health and sickness, riches and poverty, yea, all things, come not by chance but by His fatherly hand.

28.   Q. **What does it profit us to know that God has created, and by His providence still upholds, all things?**

      A. That we may be patient in adversity, thankful in prosperity, and with a view to the future may have good confidence in our faithful God and Father that no creature shall separate us from His love, since all creatures are so in His hand that without His will they cannot so much as move.

What is the providence of God? It is two things. It is first of all God's preserving or sustaining of the universe (the sum total of it, and even the smallest part). Then, second, it is God's controlling or governing of the universe so that all things work together unto that end which God has determined from the beginning.

    Both of these things are clearly revealed in the Bible. In Hebrews 1:3 we read that God is *"upholding all things by the word of His power."* And in Colossians 1:17 we read that *"in Him* [that is, in Jesus Christ] *all things consist* [or hold together]." From texts such as these we can clearly see how wrong the deists were when they compared God and the universe to a watchmaker and his watch. When a watchmaker has finished "creating" a watch, he may have nothing more to do with it (unless it breaks down and needs repair). This is not true, however, when it comes to the relationship between God and the universe. God is self-existent. The universe is not. It depends for its existence upon the upholding power of God.

It is for this reason that Paul quotes, approvingly, one of the ancient pagan poets who said concerning God that *"in Him we live and move and have our being"* (Acts 17:28).

To say that we *"live and move and have our being"* in God, however, is not to be confused with pantheism. Pantheism teaches that God is the reality of which man, nature, and the material universe are but manifestations. In a word, it says that the sum total of everything is God. But the Christian view is that God is present in the world and yet distinct from it. He sustains the universe as something distinct from himself. And yet so complete is his sovereignty over it that nothing is outside his control. Jesus said that a sparrow cannot fall to the ground unless God so determines (Matt. 10:29).

A soldier fired an arrow randomly at the enemy. A man was killed. Was it an accident from God's point of view? No, the man's death was already predicted by the Lord's prophet. So God, in reality, controlled all that happened (1 Kings 22:28, 34). What seems to us to be pure chance is really under God's government (Prov. 16:33). And, of course, so it is with all the varied forces of nature. Today there is much interest in ecology. Many of our troubles are now thought, by unbelieving men, to be due to the fact that man upsets the balance of nature. It is not our contention that there is no truth in this modern view. But we do insist that it misses the main point. The main point, according to the Bible, is that God controls the ecology of the earth. He causes things to go against man when man lives in rebellion against him (Deut. 28, the whole chapter). Conversely, when there is a turning back to God, he causes the earth to bring forth abundantly (Hos. 2:21–22). For this reason, we must beware of all relief schemes that disregard man's religious apostasy. Take, for instance, the dreadful conditions that have existed for a long time in India. Is it not plain to any Christian that as long as cows, and even rats, are reverenced as sacred, there can come no lasting improvement in the situation?

It is a great comfort to the Christian—living as he does in a world filled with problems and dangers—that God upholds and governs all that he has created. It may be that God will bring great calamities upon the world. He certainly did so in the days of Joseph the son of Jacob. We assume that every reader knows the outline of this wonderful story about the hated brother who was sold into slavery in Egypt and eventually became second only to Pharaoh (Gen. 37; 39–46). It is comforting to see in those events that God really is in control. Sometimes it is hard to see how he could be in control—as it was for Joseph and also for his father Jacob. But it was true just the same. And later on—much later on—both of them came to see it (Gen. 48:5; 50:20).

The apostle Paul tells us that *"all things work together for good to those who love God"* (Rom. 8:28). So we know that what was true in the life of Joseph—and in the life of Jacob—is also true for every believer. So, when things seem to go against us, we can remember all of the great things that God was doing for them when they were unable to see it, and we can have good confidence in our heavenly Father. This is truly one of the great comforts that belong to us as God's people.

QUESTIONS ON THE LESSON

1. What two aspects of God's work are included under the term *providence?*
2. Describe the doctrine of God held by a deist and that held by a pantheist.
3. Does God control everything that happens? Even little things? How?
4. Is there any relationship between the ecology of the earth and man's moral life? Prove it from Scripture.
5. What is the great comfort of the doctrine of providence for the believer?

QUESTIONS FOR STUDY AND DISCUSSION

1. If a person gets sick or has an accident, God is displeased with him. Is this correct thinking? Is the conclusion ever warranted that a person's misfortune is a result of his sinful living?
2. Would it be right to say that Japan is prosperous because the Japanese are living according to God's will?

3. God in his providence raises up great kings and nations. He also brings them low and destroys them. What is his purpose in all of this (cf. Dan. 4)?

Lord's Day 11

SCRIPTURE READINGS: *Colossians 2; Romans 3:9–31*

29. **Q. Why is the Son of God called *Jesus,* that is, *Savior?***
A. Because He delivers us from all our sins and saves us; and because no salvation is to be sought or found in any other.

30. **Q. Do such, then, believe in the only Savior Jesus who seek their salvation and welfare of saints, of themselves, or anywhere else?**
A. They do not; for though they boast of Him in words, yet in deeds they deny the only Savior Jesus; for one of two things must be true: either Jesus is not a complete Savior, or they who by a true faith receive this Savior must find in Him all things necessary to their salvation.

If the Bible is clear on anything, it is certainly clear on this: there is only one way of salvation. It is the way appointed by God. Yes, as the book of Proverbs truly says: *"There is a way that seems right to a man, but its end is the way of death"* (Prov. 14:12). Here is the reason. It is not man who determines what is required for salvation. No, God is the one who does this. And the central truth that he has revealed in the Bible is that the only way of salvation is the one that he provides for us.

God revealed this in principle right after the Fall, when he himself provided garments of skin for Adam and Eve (Gen. 3:21). In order to cover the nakedness of our first parents as sinners, it was necessary for some innocent animals to die. Thus, from the very beginning, *"without shedding of blood"* there could be *"no remission"* of sins (Heb. 9:22; cf. Lev. 17:11). For this reason God made a sharp distinction between the religion of Cain and the religion of Abel (Gen. 4). Cain did not bring a dying substitute as his offering, but Abel did. God had respect for Abel and his offering, but not for Cain and his offering. Why? Because there is only one way of salvation. That is all there ever has been since the fall of man. The way of salvation is through the sacrifice of an innocent victim. When that guiltless substitute dies—when the blood is shed—there is remission of sin.

But, of course, *"it is not possible that the blood of bulls and goats could take away sins"* (Heb. 10:4). The reason is rather obvious: there is no equality between them. Man is made in the image of God, but the bull or the goat is not. It is true that the bull or the goat did, under the Old Testament, suffer because of men's sin. But such animals could not, in the nature of the case, suffer the punishment due to the sinner. In order to do that, an animal would have to be able to understand the meaning of the suffering. But bulls and goats do not understand. Thus we see why the animal sacrifices of the Old Testament period had to be constantly repeated. It was necessary to keep sacrificing bulls and goats, day after day without ceasing, because these sacrifices were not enough to pay the full price of man's transgression.

The value of the animal sacrifices under the Old Testament was that they pointed to the atonement that would one day be made by the Lord Jesus. That is why God—for the time being—accepted those who came to him (as Abel did) with a bloody sacrifice. He was using this Old Testament type, or symbol, to teach his people. He was showing them by means of symbolic representation what would one day be perfectly realized in the work of the Lord Jesus. For this reason, the ceremonial law of Moses was given. In it God was showing, in great detail, the supreme importance to him of a proper sacrifice. It was for this reason, too, that when the great prophet Isaiah painted a word-picture of the future Messiah—and the sacrifice that he would make—he used the language of the ceremonial law (Isa. 53), speaking of the Messiah as a lamb led away to the slaughter.

It is also clear from this why animal sacrifices became redundant after our Lord laid down his life. When Christ died on the cross, the real atonement was made. God was at last satisfied because an adequate payment had been made. And the bloodless sacraments of baptism and the Lord's Supper replaced the bloody ceremonies of circumcision and the Passover. The Bible puts it like this: *"But this Man, after He had offered one sacrifice for sins forever, sat down at the right hand of God. . . .*

For by one offering He has perfected forever those who are being sanctified" (Heb. 10:12, 14). It is no wonder that Jesus made the claims that he did, saying, *"I am the way, the truth, and the life. No one comes to the Father except through Me"* (John 14:6). The apostle John echoed this claim when he wrote, *"He who has the Son has life; he who does not have the Son of God does not have life"* (1 John 5:12). As Peter put it in one of the early sermons of the New Testament era, *"Nor is there salvation in any other, for there is no other name under heaven given among men by which we must be saved"* (Acts 4:12).

What are we to think, then, of those who trust—in whole or in part—in something or someone other than Jesus? Is it not true today, as it was in the days when our Lord was on earth, that there are many who trust in themselves that they are righteous (Luke 18:9)? Yes, there are many today who vainly imagine that they are Christians, and yet Christ is no more to them than a great example. They really believe that God will accept them because they live by the golden rule (or so they think), or because they do the best they can! In sharp antithesis to all this, the Bible says that no one will ever be justified by his own works (Rom. 3:20).

There are also many who think they are Christians, yet they trust in others instead of, or in addition to, Jesus. Think of all those, for example, who trust in the virgin Mary or in those they call "the saints" (in the Scriptures all believers are called saints, not just a few who are regarded by men as especially holy). Today we find a rather tolerant attitude toward this evil, even among those who profess to be Reformed Christians. Yet we see no such tolerant attitude in the Bible. When the apostle John—seeing the glorious angel of God in heaven—fell down at his feet to worship, the angel said, *"See that you do not do that! I am your fellow servant, and of your brethren who have the testimony of Jesus. Worship God!"* (Rev. 19:10). It is little wonder, then, that when people fell down to worship Peter, he at once said, *"Stand up; I myself am also a man"* (Acts 10:25–26).

Can a person "really believe" in Jesus Christ while at the same time trusting in himself, or in Mary, or "the saints," or anything or anyone else? Not according to the Bible, which says that it is either the one or the other—not both, as many seem to imagine. For, as the Scripture clearly says, *"if [it is] by grace, then it is no longer of works; otherwise grace is no longer grace"* (Rom. 11:6). In other words, if you are going to have salvation as a free gift of God, then you cannot have salvation partly by merit. The one excludes the other. For *"to him who works, the wages are not counted as grace but as debt. But to him who does not work but believes on Him who justifies the ungodly, his faith is accounted for right- eousness"* (Rom. 4:4–5). As it is with trusting in Christ or in self (that is, our own "good works"), so it is with trusting in Christ or in some "saint" such as the virgin Mary. For the central principle of the Chris- tian faith is this: *"For of Him and through Him and to Him are all things,"* and therefore to him *"be glory forever"* (Rom. 11:36). The church today is in dire need of a mighty resurgence of this great truth.

QUESTIONS ON THE LESSON

1. Cite a Bible text to prove that there is only one way of salvation.
2. Why did God accept Abel but not Cain (see Heb. 11:4)?
3. The sacrificial system of the Old Testament taught two central prin- ciples. What are they?
4. What are some of the things in which people trust in addition to, or instead of, Jesus Christ?

QUESTIONS FOR STUDY AND DISCUSSION

1. Why do people easily put their trust in themselves or others but not in God?
2. Can a "good (Roman) Catholic" be saved? What reasons do you give for your answer?

LORD'S DAY 12

SCRIPTURE READINGS: *Exodus 29:1–9;*
1 Samuel 13:1–14; Romans 12:1–8

31. **Q. Why is He called *Christ,* that is, *Anointed?***
　　A. Because He is ordained of God the Father, and anointed
　　with the Holy Spirit, to be our chief Prophet and Teacher,
　　who has fully revealed to us the secret counsel and will of
　　God concerning our redemption; and our only High Priest,
　　who by the one sacrifice of His body has redeemed us, and
　　makes continual intercession for us with the Father; and our
　　eternal King, who governs us by His Word and Spirit, and
　　defends and preserves us in the salvation obtained for us.

32. **Q. But why are you called a Christian?**
　　A. Because I am a member of Christ by faith, and thus a par-
　　taker of His anointing, that I may confess His Name, pre-
　　sent myself a living sacrifice of thankfulness to Him, and
　　with a free and good conscience fight against sin and the
　　devil in this life, and hereafter reign with Him eternally
　　over all creatures.

It is a matter of common knowledge that much of the Bible has to do
with prophets, priests, and kings. Did we not, as children, begin to learn
the Bible by hearing stories about Elijah, Eli, or David? We could never
quite remember all the names of the kings of Israel and Judah. And it
was even harder to learn the names of all the different high priests. Yet
we know at least some of these men in the Old Testament who were
anointed. Think of prophets such as Elisha, Jeremiah, and Isaiah. Think

of priests such as Aaron, Abiathar, and Zachariah. Or, again, think of kings such as David, Solomon, and Josiah. Now why are they given so much prominence in the Bible?

The reason—as we see it—is that in this way God was revealing to us the purpose for which we were created. You see, we were made in the image of God. This means that man alone among the creatures was made to think God's thoughts after him. And that is not all. Man was also made to rule the world as God's servant, and in doing so to consecrate everything to God's glory.

But what is it to think God's thoughts after him? Is it not to function like a prophet? A prophet is one who speaks God's truth. And what is it to rule as God's servant? Is it not to function as a king? Likewise, to consecrate everything to God is a priestly function. So it is no exaggeration to say that man—in his original state—was supposed to function virtually as a prophet, priest, and king.

Perhaps, if man had not fallen, these functions would have been so natural to him that there never would have been any need to distinguish them. Perhaps there never would have been special offices under these names. But man did fall, and God therefore instituted these distinct offices in order that he might teach two things. The first is the complete sinfulness and inability of fallen human nature. The second thing is the kind of Savior we need. Whenever God raised up a faithful prophet, priest, or king in Old Testament times, he was revealing something of what he would one day give, perfectly, in Christ the Redeemer. And, conversely, whenever there was an unfaithful prophet, priest, or king, God was making it clear to us that no sinful man could ever measure up to his demand for perfection. Every failure was, in effect, a cry to God to send the promised Messiah. And even the best among the Old Testament prophets, priests, and kings fell so far short of that perfection that they also added to this sense of need for a heaven-sent Savior.

It is not surprising, then, that when Christ finally did come, he saw himself—and was seen by his inspired apostles—as the one who fulfilled all that was seen only to a limited degree in the best among the Old Testament prophets, priests, and kings. In the ultimate sense, the Lord Jesus Christ is the final Prophet, the final Priest, and the eternal King. We do not have priests today, in the sense of certain men appointed to this office in distinction from other men. Neither do we in the Christian church have a line of kings today. Why? Be-

cause Christ is the final son of David, who was sent to rule forever.
These three offices of the Old Testament dispensation come together,
in other words, in the person of the Lord Jesus. In him they reach their
fulfillment.

What you have in this development could be likened to the process
by which light is refracted. It is possible to take light apart, as it were,
and then put it back together. If you pass the light of the sun through
a prism, you can see the various colors of the spectrum. But if you again
intercept that spectrum with another prism of reversed polarity, the various colors will again merge. It was something like this with the image
of God. After man's fall, God began to reveal what the lost image ought
to have been. He did this through the offices of the anointed ones in
Old Testament history. Then, when the Messiah himself came, these
various "colors of the rainbow" of God's revelation were reunited in him.
He became the light of the world as the anointed one (the Christ) par
excellence.

Now it is right here that the Heidelberg Catechism gives us a wonderful insight, for it reminds us that we share in Christ's anointing. This
does not mean that every Christian has the same measure of his anointing. In John 3:34 we are expressly told that Christ did not receive the
Spirit by measure. But Christians do, for Paul says, "To each one of us
grace was given according to the measure of Christ's gift" (Eph. 4:7). We
see, then, that there is a difference between us and the Lord. And there
is also a difference between one Christian and another. Yet the wonderful thing is that something distinguishes every Christian today from
those who lived before the coming of the Savior. And that is that every
believer today shares in all these offices. Yes, this is true of even the
humblest Christian. As the Lord Jesus once said, "Assuredly, I say to you,
among those born of women there has not risen one greater than John the
Baptist; but he who is least in the kingdom of heaven is greater than he"
(Matt. 11:11).

Now what does this statement mean? It cannot possibly mean that
every Christian today is more pious or faithful than John. If we are honest, we will not make any such claim for ourselves. No, what our Lord
means is that the time has now arrived in the history of salvation in
which we—at last—can share in all three of these offices with our Savior. John the Baptist could not do this. Under the Old Testament it was
a great sin for any king, for example, to intrude in any way into the
priestly function (see 1 Sam. 13:1–14).

It is not our intention here to give anything more than a few suggestive thoughts about the greatness of our present advantage. But we do offer a few reminders of what we now have as a consequence of the saving work of Jesus. We have God's complete word in the Bible. That is more than any of the Old Testament prophets ever possessed. We also have the privilege of coming boldly into the very presence of our heavenly Father (Heb. 4:16). Even the high priest of Israel could never do that. He could only come once each year into the Holy of Holies. We can come whenever we desire, as long as we come in the merits and through the mediation of Christ. And what about our kingly position? In the Old Testament period, the kings of Israel ruled over one tiny nation—the nation of Israel. But we are called to rule the whole world for God's glory and honor (Matt. 28:18–20; Rom. 16:20; 1 Cor. 15:25–28). It is no wonder that Peter says we *"are a chosen generation, a royal priesthood, a holy nation, His own special people"* (1 Peter 2:9). And it is all because we really do share in Christ's anointing. It is for this reason that Reformed Christians have always stressed the fact that Christ, alone, is the supreme ruler of the church. Under him no mere man (such as the pope) can lord it over others. Yet we all have a share in the ruling power of the church (think of Matt. 18:15–18). That is why Reformed Christians reject the very thought of any special priestly order in the church. We believe in the priesthood of believers, in which we all have the high privilege of intercession for one another through the sole mediation of Christ, our only high priest.

And this is only the beginning! We will never cease to be prophets, priests, and kings in union with and in submission to the Messiah. Through all eternity we will continue to share these offices with him. It really is a wonderful thing to bear the name of Christ! The very name *Christian* means that we partake of his anointing!

QUESTIONS ON THE LESSON

1. Why are the prophets, priests, and kings so prominently featured in the Old Testament?
2. What did God teach through these special offices in the Old Testament?
3. Why did these special offices cease under the New Testament?
4. Contrast the true and false interpretations of Matthew 11:11.

QUESTIONS FOR STUDY AND DISCUSSION

1. Use a Bible dictionary to find the Hebrew equivalent for the title "Christ."
2. Did Jesus hold the offices of Prophet, Priest, and King right from the time he was born, or did he receive these offices at some later time? What significance does Matthew 3:16–17 have in answering this question?
3. What does the letter to the church in Thyatira (Rev. 2:18–29) indicate about the kingly office of believers?
4. What prophetic functions do believers perform today? What priestly functions? What kingly functions?
5. Does God trust us enough to give us real authority as prophets, priests, and kings? Would you trust yourself with such authority? Why does God?

LORD'S DAY 13

SCRIPTURE READINGS: *Isaiah 7:10–14; 9:1–7;*
Hebrews 2:5–18

33. **Q.** **Why is He called God's *only begotten Son,* since we also
are children of God?**

A. Because Christ alone is the eternal, natural Son of God;
but we are children of God by adoption, through grace, for
Christ's sake.

34. **Q.** **Why do you call Him *our Lord?***

A. Because He has redeemed us, body and soul, from all our
sins, not with gold or silver, but with His precious blood,
and has delivered us from all the power of the devil, and
has made us His own possession.

Young believers are sometimes confused when they hear that Jesus is
God's only begotten Son, and also that they too are God's children.
What they need to understand is that there are two kinds of children!
The children in a family may have been born to the parents or they
may have been adopted by them. Sometimes it even happens that a
couple will adopt one or two children and then have one or two natural children.

Adoption is a wonderful thing. A child who had nothing, as it
were, suddenly has "everything"—a home, security, even the same legal
rights as naturally born children. Perhaps you have seen the beauty of
children who have been adopted by Christian parents. Yet adopted children do not always realize it! I once knew a man who—during World
War II—found out that he was adopted. (Incidentally, it is our convic-

tion that parents should never keep this information from their adopted children.) Well, when he found out that he was adopted, he became obsessed with the desire to find out about his natural parents. But when he did, something wonderful happened. He suddenly realized that his "real" parents did not mean nearly so much to him as his adoptive parents! He realized, as never before, how much he owed them, and that he loved them a thousand times more than he could possibly love two people who had abandoned him.

Well, our relationship with the heavenly Father is something like that. You see, Jesus is the only begotten Son of God. We could say that he was—and is—God's only "natural" Son. We, on the other hand, are the "natural" sons of Adam. We come from parents who descended from Adam. Because Adam fell and yielded his heart to the mastery of Satan, there is also a sense in which we have to say that Satan is also our natural father. But what happens when we are brought by the power of the Holy Spirit to believe the gospel? What happens when we come to faith and repentance? Well, what happens is that God adopts us. He makes us part of his household. We become heirs of God and joint heirs with Christ in all that the Father gives him.

From all this we learn, first of all, that the Lord Jesus is divine. We see that he is no less than God. This is evident from the fact that God is infinite, eternal, and unchangeable. If this be true, then God the Father was always the Father. And how could he be the Father eternally unless his Son is eternal, too? It is in this sense that he is God's child in a way that we never can be. We are God's children because God had compassion on us, chose us, and adopted us. But for the Lord Jesus Christ this was a matter of birthright. There never was a time—from all eternity—that Jesus was not begotten. We are all begotten in time. We all have a beginning. But it is exactly this that we do not have in mind when we speak of God's only begotten Son Jesus.

Theologians have sometimes tried to explain what it means that Christ was eternally begotten. One of them, Jonathan Edwards (as we recall), put it something like this: God the Father, being infinite, eternal, and unchangeable, had an infinite, eternal, and unchangeable idea of himself! This infinite, eternal, and unchangeable idea of himself was "the Word." And the Bible says, *In the beginning was the Word, and the Word was with God, and the Word was God*" (John 1:1). Now God the Father loved his "eternal Word" (his only begotten Son) with a love that was also infinite, eternal, and unchangeable. And this, in turn, came back to God the Father from his only begotten Son. Edwards then said that this infinite, eternal, and unchanging love must be the Holy Spirit (and it is indeed true that the Bible says God is love). Well, it is a good question whether or not such speculations are helpful or harmful. We simply do not know—because God has not revealed to us the mystery of Christ's eternal generation by the Father. What we do know for sure is that the inspired Scriptures tell us that Christ is God's only begotten Son. His divine nature was eternally generated by the Father.

It is important to stress that when we speak of Christ as God's only begotten Son, we are not thinking about his conception or birth as a human being. As we will see in the next lesson, Christ was also very different from us in the manner of his human birth. He alone was conceived in a virgin's womb and born without a human father. But what is meant here is that our Lord was divine (in the highest possible sense) before he was human. We call him Lord—as the Catechism says—because he is our Redeemer. With his own precious blood he has paid for our sins, so that we can become the adopted sons of his Father. But when we call him Lord, in the biblical sense of that word, we are recognizing his divine nature. In the Old Testament, God made himself known to his covenant people by the name *Yahweh* (*Jehovah*), which we translate as "Lord" (Ex. 3:13–15). And in the New Testament that name is applied to Jesus our Savior (John 8:58). When Thomas fell at the feet of Jesus, making his great confession (John 20:28), he was confessing Jesus to be nothing less than Jehovah, the God of the Old Testament Scriptures. Because Jesus was divine, in the highest sense of that word, as well as truly human, Thomas could bow before him and say to him, "*My Lord [or Jehovah] and my God!*" How the divine Son became man will be our subject in the next lesson.

QUESTIONS ON THE LESSON

1. What are the two types of human sonship?
2. How do they differ?
3. In what ways are they alike?
4. Who is the natural father of all men?
5. What is the most difficult thing for us to understand about the sonship of Christ?
6. What does the confession of Thomas (John 20:28) prove?

QUESTIONS FOR STUDY AND DISCUSSION

1. Using a concordance, find Scripture passages that show that believers have a right to inherit God's blessings as his true sons.
2. What is the significance of God's name *Jehovah* (meaning "I am")? A commentary on Exodus 3:13–15 may help.

LORD'S DAY 14

SCRIPTURE READINGS: *Psalm 110;*
Matthew 1:1–25; Luke 1:26–55

35. **Q. What does it mean that He was *conceived by the Holy Spirit, born of the virgin Mary?***

A. That God's eternal Son, who is and continues true and eternal God, took upon Himself the very nature of man of the flesh and blood of the virgin Mary, by the operation of the Holy Spirit, that He might also be the true seed of David, like unto His brethren in all things, sin excepted.

36. **Q. What benefit do you receive from the holy conception and birth of Christ?**

A. That He is our Mediator, and with His innocence and perfect holiness covers, in the sight of God, my sin wherein I was conceived and brought forth.

Did you ever find the Bible a bit monotonous to read? We sometimes have this reaction to passages in which we find a genealogical record. Perhaps that is why we seldom, if ever, hear a sermon expounding one of these passages (such as Gen. 5). Yet there are instances in which God uses precisely such material in the Bible to bring people to see their need of the Savior. The story is told, for instance, of a man who was listening to a minister reading the fifth chapter of Genesis. He began to notice that throughout the account of the people who lived before the great Flood, each entry ended with the words "and he died." Suddenly it dawned on him, as never before, that this is our human condition. We are born, we live for a time, and then—sooner or later—death takes us. When he saw this, he realized his need for a Savior—someone who could bring life back to the dead and dying.

But how could this sad condition be changed? And who had the resources to do it? This is the question that God answered for us when he sent his eternal Son to assume human nature. But how could the Son of God become man, so that he could be both divine and human? Truly, this was one of the great mysteries of the Old Testament revelation, a mystery that no one could fathom. We can see this clearly from a question that Jesus put to the Jews who were offended by the claims he was making. Because he claimed to be God's Son, they said that he was claiming to be God's equal. They were basically right about that— he did say he was God's equal (John 5:19–30). He also asked two questions that put the whole thing in focus. The first question was: "*What do you think about the Christ? Whose son is He?*" They answered, "*The Son of David*" (Matt. 22:42). This was, of course, the right answer. But then Jesus asked a second question: "*How then does David in the Spirit call Him 'Lord'? . . . If David then calls Him 'Lord,' how is He his Son?*" (Matt. 22:43–45). This question they could not answer.

But the answer is provided for us in the New Testament—particularly in the gospel accounts of Luke and of Matthew. According to these two gospels, there was a young unmarried girl named Mary, who was engaged to a man known as Joseph. She had not had sexual relations with Joseph (or with any other man), and yet she became pregnant. When Joseph found out that Mary was pregnant, he assumed that she had been unfaithful. He would have ended their plans for marriage right then and there if it had not been for divine intervention. An angel of God came to Joseph and made it clear to him—as he had earlier made it clear to Mary—that it was God himself, rather than some man, who had caused Mary to become pregnant. So Joseph took Mary to be his wife, but did not have sexual relations with her until after the birth of Jesus.

What happened was explained by the angel of God, when he said this to Mary: "*The Holy Spirit will come upon you, and the power of the Highest will overshadow you; therefore, also, that Holy One who is to be born will be called the Son of God*" (Luke 1:35). It does not belong to us to know more than this about this great miracle of Christ's conception. It is enough for us to know that the power of God was sufficient to enable Mary to conceive in her womb a child with no human father. In this way our Savior could be both divine and human—sharing the very nature of God, and yet sharing also our flesh and blood, derived through the virgin Mary. If Jesus had been born of a human father and mother, then he would have shared in Adam's fallen nature. But precisely because this was not the case, he did not share in Adam's transgression. His human nature was brought into existence, in other words, in a special—supernatural—manner, so that he could be both God and man, and sinless as to his human nature.

Some years ago, in a seminary classroom, there was a heated argument about whether the doctrine of the virgin birth of Christ is essential for our salvation. The argument was inconclusive because the two sides approached the question from quite different perspectives. One side was asking the question from a desire to know how much we must know and believe in order to be saved. And from that standpoint, the answer is negative. The thief on the cross was saved, but he probably did not know (and consequently could not believe) the doctrine of the virgin birth of Christ. The others in the argument wanted to know exactly what nature Christ had to have in order to save us. From their standpoint, the doctrine of the virgin birth of Christ is essential. We could not have been saved without a Savior who (1) shared our human nature, (2) yet did not share in the sin of our nature, and (3) also had the infinite power to do the great work of salvation that was needed.

There are two distinct issues here. We must be sure we do not confuse them. God can save a man with a limited grasp of the truth, but we can in no way reduce the content of the truth to be apprehended.

The only salvation that the Bible speaks of is the salvation we find in Jesus, and the only Jesus who really exists is the one "conceived by the Holy Spirit" of God and "born of the virgin Mary." The more we read the gospel accounts—and come to know their portrait of Christ—the more we see how this doctrine is essential to our understanding of Jesus. How else can we explain one thing that was testified to by all who came to know him? There was no sin—no evil thing—no charge that anyone could justly bring against him. Even Pilate, who gave him over to a terrible death, admitted that he was blameless (John 18:38). The thing that should make the greatest impression of all is the fact that even his closest disciples—who were with him day after day, even with him in times of crisis—unanimously agreed that he was sinless. Now, how could this be, if Jesus was man (and about that there can be no question)? How was it possible, unless he was different from the beginning? Is it not clear that the record is right when it speaks of his miraculous conception?

Because this doctrine is true, we have the answer to our number one problem. Here, at last, is one who can take my sin and guilt and remove it all from God's sight forever. In that sense, the doctrine of the virgin conception of Christ is absolutely essential. We have a Savior only because he really was born in this way.

QUESTIONS ON THE LESSON

1. What is so remarkable about David's statement in Psalm 110:1?
2. What was unique about the birth of Jesus Christ?
3. Is the doctrine of Christ's virgin birth essential for salvation?

QUESTIONS FOR STUDY AND DISCUSSION

1. Biologically, what miraculous events occurred in the conception of Jesus?
2. Why do so many people have trouble accepting the doctrine of the virgin birth of Christ?

LORD'S DAY 15

SCRIPTURE READINGS: *John 17; 10:1–30*

37. Q. What does it mean that He *suffered*?

A. That all the time He lived on earth, but especially at the end of His life, He bore, in body and soul, the wrath of God against the sin of the whole human race, in order that by His passion, as the only atoning sacrifice, He might redeem our body and soul from everlasting damnation and obtain for us the grace of God, righteousness, and eternal life.

38. Q. Why did He suffer *under Pontius Pilate* as judge?

A. That He, though innocent, might be condemned by a temporal judge, and thereby free us from the severe judgment of God to which we were subject.

39. Q. Is there anything more in His having been *crucified* than if He had died some other death?

A. Yes, since thereby I am assured that He took on Himself the curse which lay upon me; for the death of the cross was accursed of God.

The whole life of our Lord involved suffering. He was with the Father before the world was made. Even if he had become a man before the Fall, it still would have been a great act of self-abasement. For the Creator to have "come down" to the level of the creature would have been an amazing thing in itself, even if sin did not exist. But when Christ actually did come, the human race had fallen, and sin and evil prevailed

in the world. Yet, in spite of this fact, he came. And who can understand the magnitude of the self-abasement involved? All men, to a
greater or lesser extent, experience sorrow and suffering. Yet, for us, it
is not a matter of choice. We come into existence, not by our own will,
but by the will of others (our parents and—ultimately—God). But with
Jesus it was not so. He came into the human race by his own choice
(though, of course, also by God's sovereign will), and he did it in order
that he might deal with the cause of our alienation from God. All men
were created in Adam. They also fell with him in his first transgression.
Therefore, the anger of God rested upon all men as fallen.

It was to deal with this problem that Christ came. He came in order to give himself as a sacrifice to satisfy divine justice. And to this
end he did two things: First, he rendered active obedience to God. That
is, he kept all of God's commandments perfectly. He did this from the
beginning to the end of his earthly life. Not once did any of his disciples find any sin in him. Neither did Christ himself ever confess any
sin. And that is not all: even the Father in heaven saw no sin in him,
for he said, *"This is My beloved Son, in whom I am well pleased"* (Matt.
3:17). The second thing that Jesus did was to render passive obedience.
This means that he received the entire punishment due for the sins of
his people. He suffered their condemnation in full measure. He did this
when he was beaten, smitten, and afflicted—and, above all, when he
was crucified.

It is very important to note that the atonement of Christ does not
benefit all people without exception. This is not what the Catechism
means when it says that Christ "bore . . . the wrath of God against the
sin of the whole human race." This phrase means that the anger of
God, which came down upon our Savior, was not a wrath different
from the wrath that will come down upon those who are lost on the
Last Day. No, it is the same wrath. It is the wrath of utter damnation.
But it is only a portion of "the whole human race" for which Jesus
died—namely, those who were given to him by his heavenly Father.
We know this because Jesus said so. In John 17 we have his "high
priestly prayer," which he prayed just before he was crucified. In this
prayer he made it clear that the design of his suffering was not the salvation of all men, but only of that portion of the human race that had
been given to him by his Father. Here is what he said: *"I do not pray
for the world but for those whom You have given Me, for they are Yours"*
(v. 9). Christ died as a substitute for these people, not for all men with-

out exception. That is what the Catechism has in mind when it says that he died "in order that . . . He might redeem our body and soul from everlasting damnation and obtain for us the grace of God, righteousness, and eternal life." The word "us" simply means the people of God—those who are true believers.

"The authorities that exist are appointed by God," according to the apostle Paul (Rom. 13:1). This means that Pontius Pilate was there by God's sovereign appointment. It was no accident that the great Roman Empire then held sway over Israel, and that the Son of God was born on this earth under that government. It was also no accident that the trial of Jesus was held before this civil ruler, who first said, "I find no fault in this man," and then delivered him up to be cruelly punished— first by a horrible flogging and then by an even more terrible death! In this way the almighty God, who controls all things on the earth and causes them to work together to accomplish his purpose, brought the salient facts to public notice. It is a matter of public record, in other words, that there was no fault in the Lord Jesus, and that he was nevertheless given the sentence of the death reserved for reprobate people. The apostle Paul put it like this: *"He made Him who knew no sin to be sin for us, that we might become the righteousness of God in Him"* (2 Cor. 5:21).

In the Old Testament it is stated that *"he who is hanged is accursed of God"* (Deut. 21:23). The context shows that Moses was speaking of what was to be done with someone who was executed for a capital crime. The corpse of such a person was not to be left hanging all night, since that would defile the land. That is, it would render the land odious to God. Evidently the wicked person, who was thus to be executed, was to be removed from God's sight, as it were. And it was through the providence of God that Jesus was subjected to the execution reserved for such people. Because we see God's hand in all this, we are more convinced that he died as a substitute for lost sinners. And knowing this, we can rest assured that what he did for us was more than sufficient.

The design of the suffering and death of Jesus was not the salvation of all men. But we must never forget that the value of Jesus' sacrifice is absolutely infinite. What Christ suffered was more than enough to save the whole human race. For this reason, no one need ever fear any insufficiency in the saving power of the precious blood of Christ. It is more than sufficient to save even the greatest of sinners, and so all who come to Jesus by faith shall have eternal salvation.

QUESTIONS ON THE LESSON

1. In what sense did Christ sustain "the wrath of God against the sin of the whole human race"?
2. What false construction, sometimes placed on these words, is to be avoided?
3. What is meant by Christ's active obedience?
4. What is meant by his passive obedience?
5. Quote words from John 17 that prove that it was not Christ's intention, or design, to save all men by his death.
6. Why was it important for Christ to be executed by civil authority?
7. Why was it necessary for him to be crucified?

QUESTIONS FOR STUDY AND DISCUSSION

1. Why do many people hold to the false idea that Christ intended to die for all men?
2. If Christ intended to die for all men, then either he did not accomplish what he intended to do (since some men are lost) or else all men are actually saved. Discuss the implications of each of these consequences of this false view.
3. What great comfort can believers take from the truth that Christ's death for them was effective (i.e., that he accomplished what he intended, namely, actually saving his people)?

LORD'S DAY 16

SCRIPTURE READINGS: *2 Thessalonians 1:3–12;*
Romans 3:19–28; Mark 9:38–50

40. **Q. Why was it necessary for Christ to humble Himself even
unto *death?***
A. Because, by reason of the justice and truth of God, satisfaction for our sins could be made no otherwise than by
the death of the Son of God.

41. **Q. Why was He *buried?***
A. To prove thereby that He was really dead.

42. **Q. Since, then, Christ died for us, why must we also die?**
A. Our death is not a satisfaction for our sins, but only a dying to sins and entering into eternal life.

43. **Q. What further benefit do we receive from the sacrifice
and death of Christ on the cross?**
A. That by His power our old man is crucified, slain, and
buried with Him, that so the evil lusts of the flesh may no
more reign in us, but that we may offer ourselves unto Him
a sacrifice of thanksgiving.

44. **Q. Why is there added, *He descended into hell?***
A. That in my greatest temptations I may be assured, and
wholly comfort myself with this, that my Lord Jesus Christ,
by His inexpressible anguish, pains, terrors, and hellish

agony in which He was plunged during all His sufferings, but especially on the cross, has delivered me from the anguish and torment of hell.

Was the death of Christ really necessary? Was there no other way that God could save us? To such questions as these there can be but one answer: there was no other way. Christ had to die in order for us to be saved. The reason for this is found in the very nature of God. He is holy and righteous. There is no way that God could possibly bypass the demands of justice. How, then, could he allow sinners to go free? How could he treat them as if they had never sinned? Well, one thing is certain—he could not do it by allowing sin to go unpunished. To do that, God would have to deny himself, and the Scripture says that God cannot do that. We see, then, that God's own perfect nature requires either that he punish us for what we have done, or that he allow a substitute to stand in our place and receive our punishment for us. And that is exactly what Jesus did in order to save his people.

And what was the punishment required by God's own righteous nature? The answer, of course, is "death." This was made clear at the very beginning of human history, when God warned our first parents that the wages of sin is death—and by this, of course, he meant an eternal death. Death does not mean nonexistence. It means eternal existence away from God and away from all of the blessings that come from God. It has to be eternal because sin against an infinite God requires an infinite penalty. The only way a finite creature can pay an infinite penalty is to keep on paying it forever. But here is the good news: because Jesus is infinite (being divine) as well as finite (being human), he was able to suffer the infinite penalty in a finite period of time. He suffered only for a time, but because he was infinite, he was able to suffer an infinite amount. As a matter of fact, his suffering was the equivalent of eternal damnation. Therefore, he is able to save us from eternal death.

But, of course, the question naturally arises: why do we still have to die if Jesus died in our place? It is our conviction that the main reason for our problem here is an incorrect idea of death. We tend to think of death as the separation of body and spirit. And it is true enough that this is what the word *death* is commonly used to denote. However, in the Bible *death* is a much wider concept. It includes the separation of soul and body, but it also includes much more. When

God threatened our first parents, he said, *"In the day that you eat of it dying you shall die"* (Gen. 2:17, NKJV margin). So it is in the Hebrew, and such is the truth of the matter. That is why the natural man is referred to in the Bible as *"dead in trespasses and sins"* (Eph. 2:1). Death, in the most fundamental sense, is separation from God and from all that man was created to possess in God. Thus, death in fact began, for Adam and Eve, as soon as they ate the forbidden fruit. But it did not end there. Later on, Adam and Eve also had to experience the separation of body and spirit. But even that is not all. Death is not completed until the whole man—body and soul—is cast into outer darkness on the great day of God's judgment, when there will be weeping and wailing and gnashing of teeth.

The salvation that is granted to God's people, on the other hand, is also a process. It is a step-by-step progression out of the realm of death and into the possession of life. It begins when the spirit (or soul) is quickened (or made alive again) by the Holy Spirit. This is the first resurrection. *"Blessed and holy is he who has part in the first resurrection. Over such the second* [i.e., final] *death has no power"* (Rev. 20:6). So the Christian, having been renewed in heart or soul (1 John 3:4), already has the beginning of eternal life in him. But the physical body does not yet participate in the resurrection life. No, the body continues to be a body of sin and death (as Paul reminds us in Romans 7:24). Now, of course, God could have given us renewed bodies at the same time that he gave us renewed souls. But he did not. Rather, he determined that this would not be ours until the Last Day. Perhaps the main reason for this is that we can thus continue to live together in the same society with (as yet) unregenerate men. A believing wife, for instance, can continue to live with an unbelieving husband—and who knows but that he too may yet be converted (1 Peter 3:1–2). If we passed out of death into life in such a way that we were instantly finished products, we could not dwell together in the same society with the dead. For the Christian believer, physical death is really just one further step into life. Why? Because the *"spirits of just men"* are *"made perfect"* at death (Heb. 12:23). When this happens, the body of sin and death can no longer influence the spirit (or soul) toward evil. But that is not all, for believers. In their case even the body remains united to Christ, in the grave, as it awaits the Resurrection. So our experience of the last aspect of death with which we have to do—namely, the separation of soul and body—is not in any sense, for us, a punishment for sin. Christ has taken care of that. It is simply the next to last phase of our progress out of death and into life. The last phase will come when the physical body is raised up on the Last Day in the likeness of our Lord's own glorious body.

You can see, then, what tremendous comfort there is in knowing that Jesus died on the cross for his people. As a matter of fact, that death was not his alone. No, because of the corporate solidarity existing between Jesus Christ and his people (and remember, it is like the old corporate solidarity that exists between fallen Adam and his people), it is really true that we died with him and also have risen to newness of life. On the one hand, in other words, there is the representative principle—Christ acting for, or on behalf of, his people. But, on the other hand, there is the principle of vital union—Christ actually communicating a renewed human nature to those for whom he has acted. The same Holy Spirit that dwells in him without measure also dwells in us. And we really are new creatures made after the likeness of Jesus.

There is no phrase in the Apostles' Creed that has caused so much difficulty as this: "He descended into hell." Also, there is disagreement as to what the ancient church meant when it included these words in this earliest Christian confession. Yet in spite of the difficulty, the church has never been willing to remove these words. How then shall we understand them? We cannot possibly take these words to mean that Christ, after he died, went to the place where lost men go to suffer forever. We know he did not go there because he told the believing thief who died at his side that he would be with him that very day in paradise (Luke 23:43). The biblical meaning must be that what Christ suffered on the cross was itself a descent into hell. Now at first sight it might seem ridiculous to say that Jesus, in a few hours of suffering, could have experienced hell to the fullest. But remember, he was divine as well as human. Remember, too, that his human nature was sinless. Just imagine how great the suffering must have been for him when he was forsaken by God. Yes, because of the uniqueness of Jesus Christ, it was possible for him to suffer the full measure of the infinite wrath and curse of God—what damnation is for the wicked. And because he did, you and I can be sure that God's justice is fully satisfied, so that we shall escape that damnation. Here is the Christian's solid basis for hope.

Is there really a hell? Look at the cross of Christ and you will know the answer. But that is not all: if you look in faith, you will also know that Jesus will never let you experience that horror.

Questions on the Lesson

1. Why was the death of Christ necessary?
2. How could Christ pay an infinite price in a brief period of time?
3. What is wrong with the common concept of death?
4. What does the word *death* mean according to Scripture?
5. Why has God determined that our bodies, for the present, remain bodies of death?
6. What do we mean when we say that "the death that Jesus died on the cross was not his death alone"?
7. What does the phrase "He descended into hell" mean?
8. What is the strongest proof of the reality of hell?

Questions for Study and Discussion

1. Consider what Christ meant when he uttered from the cross that terrible cry, "*My God, My God, why have You forsaken Me?*" (Matt. 27:46). What does this tell us about the nature of God's judgment?
2. The so-called Spiritualist Church teaches that man has an immortal soul that can never die. They offer as evidence the communications they claim to have received from those who have died. In these communications they are taught that there is no such thing as hell. What is the biblical response to this lie of Satan?
3. If there is no hell, man is forced to accept one of two ideas. Either death is annihilation (which is taught by the Jehovah's Witnesses) or there is no final justice for the deeds of men—Hitler and Stalin will dwell in the realm of the dead on the same level as the most humble and pious believer! Why are both of these ideas unacceptable to the true believer?

LORD'S DAY 17

SCRIPTURE READINGS: *1 Corinthians 15:1–28;*
John 5:19–29

45.   Q. **What does the *resurrection* of Christ profit us?**
 A. First, by His resurrection He has overcome death, that He
 might make us partakers of the righteousness which He has
 obtained for us by His death; second, we also are raised up
 by His power to a new life; and third, the resurrection of
 Christ is to us a sure pledge of our blessed resurrection.

We need to be specific. What do we mean when we speak of Christ's
resurrection? The biblical answer is that the dead body of Jesus came
back to life again. Yes, it is true that when Christ rose up again, his body
was different in its qualities. But it was still the very same body in identity. That is why the scars were still visible. There are some theologians
today, however, who say we cannot possibly take the reports of the disciples as literally true in our scientific age. The reason, they say, is that
we now have scientific knowledge that human bodies just do not get up
again after they are dead. Thus, it has become common today to treat
the account of Christ's resurrection as mythical or symbolic. I once heard
a theologian expressing this view in a TV interview. He began by saying, "I believe in the resurrection of Jesus." That sounded fine, of course,
but one of the TV interviewers realized that what this man had in mind
was not what many of the listeners might imagine. So he asked him one
simple question: "Would you also say that Karl Marx is risen?" The theologian was cornered, but in this case he was also honest. So he said
yes. Thus it suddenly became clear that in this man's theology, words
were being given new meanings. *Resurrection* no longer meant for him

the raising up of dead bodies. No, for him it simply meant that "the spirit of a man will live on—in other people—through his teaching." Well, that is not at all what the Bible means when it speaks of resurrection. No, what the Bible means by this word is that dead bodies stand up again. And the disciples wrote the report about this because it actually happened.

Now, of course, we can't help but wonder how such a miracle could happen. And the answer today is exactly the same as it was in the days of the disciples. We don't know how dead bodies can be restored to life again, but is it not true that God can do all sorts of things that we can't explain? As a matter of fact, is it not true that there are things in our everyday experience that no one can fathom? For example, how can a thought in my mind result in the movement of my whole body? The answer is that we don't really know how. But it does happen. Why, then, should it be thought incredible for God—or the Son of God—to do other things that man cannot figure out? We believe it is important to emphasize this, because no one can be an authentic Christian who does not believe in the God who works wonders. There is no such thing as authentic Christian faith without acceptance of the bodily resurrection of Jesus. We must be honest. If this is not what really happened, then what good does it do to be Christians? A "savior" who cannot deliver from death is worse than no savior at all. On the other hand, what if these things actually did happen? Well, then it is clear that the disciples were right in thinking they had a message that everyone needed— a message of world-shaking importance. It is to this fact that the Catechism here draws our attention.

If Christ really did get up out of his grave, then there is—at last— an answer to man's ultimate problem: the problem of death. If he really arose, then death has been conquered. It can never again be looked on as final—as the "last word"—by the people of Jesus. Why? Because he has promised that his glorious experience we will experience also. And that is not all. As a matter of fact, we already have a kind of down payment—or first installment—of what the Scripture calls the first resurrection. The first resurrection is more often called regeneration. It is the act of God, through the Holy Spirit, by which we become new creatures. The believer, in other words, already partakes of the new life that belongs to Christ by virtue of his resurrection. And this, in turn, is the guarantee of the second installment. The second installment, which will be given to us on the Last Day at the return of Christ, will be the raising up from the grave of our physical bodies. In other words, our spirits (or souls) already participate in the resurrection life of the Lord Jesus. And our bodies will one day undergo a similar transition. Our bodies are going to stand on this earth again at the return of the Lord.

QUESTIONS ON THE LESSON

1. What do some apostate theologians mean by the term *resurrection?*
2. What does the Bible mean by the term?
3. Why is this doctrine essential to authentic Christianity?
4. What is the first resurrection? What is the second resurrection?

QUESTIONS FOR STUDY AND DISCUSSION

1. Many people have noted that there are a number of similarities between God's initial creation of man from the dust of the earth and his resurrection of men from the dead on the Last Day. Discuss the similarities and differences that you find between creation and resurrection.
2. If a person's body is completely obliterated, and then that person is raised from the dead, can he really be considered the same person? What continuity is there that allows us to think of this person as actually the same person?
3. The Spiritualist Church teaches that man's soul is eternal. How is this different from Christian teaching?
4. There are many theological terms whose precise meanings have been established over a long history of Christian usage—e.g., *Christian, redemption, born again, revival, holy, Christ.* Discuss the historic Christian meanings of these terms and compare them to contemporary redefinitions.

Lord's Day 18

SCRIPTURE READINGS: *Acts 1:1–11;*
Colossians 1:13–23; 1 Corinthians 15:25–28

46. Q. **How do you understand the words,** *He ascended into heaven?*

A. That Christ, in the sight of His disciples, was taken up from earth into heaven, and there continues for our interest, until He comes again to judge the living and the dead.

47. Q. **Is Christ, then, not with us even to the end of the world, as He has promised?**

A. Christ is true man and true God: with respect to His human nature, He is no more on earth; but with respect to His Godhead, majesty, grace, and Spirit, He is at no time absent from us.

48. Q. **But if His human nature is not present wherever His Godhead is, are not then these two natures in Christ separated from one another?**

A. Not at all; for since the Godhead is illimitable and omnipresent, it must follow that it is beyond the bounds of the human nature it has assumed, and yet none the less is in this human nature and remains personally united to it.

49. Q. **Of what advantage to us is Christ's ascension into heaven?**

A. First, that He is our Advocate in the presence of His Father in heaven; second, that we have our flesh in heaven

> as a sure pledge that He, as the Head, will also take us,
> His members, up to Himself; third, that He sends us His
> Spirit as an earnest, by whose power we *seek the things that
> are above, where Christ is, seated on the right hand of God,
> and not the things that are upon the earth.*

The word *resurrection* is not the only one that is misrepresented today. The word *ascension* is also. For many today, this word means little more than some kind of survival of the spirit after the death of the body. It is said that people are too sophisticated today to accept the biblical story of Christ's ascension as something that actually happened. No, they say, it is simply the way in which prescientific men expressed their inner experience. And what was that inner experience? Well, it was that somehow Jesus still lived. And how would a prescientific man express that? Well, they say, he would express it in terms of his primitive cosmology. And what was that? It was the idea that the universe is divided into three portions: with heaven "up there," hell "down below," and the earth in the middle. So these men tried to express what they had experienced, by saying that Jesus had ascended into heaven.

But stop and think for a moment. Is this really convincing? We all know today that the world is round, and that heaven surrounds the entire planet outward (you could say) in every direction. Yes, but what do we see and hear on television, when one of our rocket ships zooms into space? Well, we see it going up. Even sophisticated scientists stand there and watch as it goes up and is received out of sight by the clouds. And on the evening news they tell us not only that it went "up" but also when it will come "down." How clear it is, then, that the report of the disciples of Christ was not expressed in the way it was because these men were prescientific. No, it was expressed that way because that is always the way it looks when someone departs from this planet. And the simple fact is that our Lord Jesus Christ did depart from this planet. He went up—and away—from the earth to some other place in the universe, in order to prepare a place for his people. When the set time comes, he will return. He will come down again from what we still call heaven, to be with his people.

We know that Jesus is no longer here, on the earth, because he has gone to be with the Father. He is now reigning at the right hand of God, and he will keep on reigning until he has put all enemies under his feet (and all enemies of his people, including death). The last enemy is death, and death too will be utterly vanquished. This will take place on the Last Day, when Jesus comes to judge all men, living and dead, both the righteous and the wicked. It is for this reason that we cannot agree with some of the sentiments we hear today concerning "the presence of Jesus." There is, indeed, a sense in which Jesus is now with his people (and will be, to the end of the ages). But he is not now present with them in the same way that he was before the Ascension, or as he shall be after the Second Coming. The person of Jesus, the God-man, is at this present time absent from the world. The angel said to those who sought Jesus at the tomb, *"He is not here; for He is risen"* (Matt. 28:6), and we must say the same thing today—that Jesus is not here in his human nature (as he was here for forty days after the Resurrection). But he will be here when he comes again on the Last Day of this era.

On the one hand, then, it is important to stress the fact that Jesus is present with us today through the person and work of the Holy Spirit. As a matter of fact, it is the great work of the Holy Spirit (in and by means of the written Word of God) to take the things of the Lord Jesus Christ and reveal them to us. Just as Jesus could say to his disciples, *"He who has seen Me has seen the Father"* (John 14:9), so we can say today, "He who has the Holy Spirit dwelling in his heart also has Jesus with him." On the other hand, we must also be clear that there is a big difference between the spiritual presence of Christ that we have now and the physical presence by which our Lord will one day again be with us in the future. To confuse the two is to misunderstand the nature of the Ascension.

There is a false piety—all too common today—which reflects just this confusion. You hear it in songs that pretend that we can meet Jesus walking in the garden while the dew is still on the roses. We hear it in sermons that reduce the message of the resurrected and ascended Christ to a little Jesus who "lives in my heart." (Yes, of course, there is—or at least can be—an element of truth in this. But what we are talking about is reducing the gospel to this small dimension. What is important is not so much that Jesus lives in me, as that Jesus sits at the right hand of the Father and from there rules in me by his Spirit). We should by all means be thankful that our Lord Jesus is with us (in the person and work of the Holy Spirit) even to the end of the age. But there would be no comfort at all, if we did not know—at the same time—that one day he will return and that we will see him in all of his glory with our very own eyes. And that moment, too, will be just as literal and historical as the Resurrection and the Ascension.

Jesus Christ is not with us in the same way that he was with his disciples for forty days after his resurrection. But he is with us and will continue to be until the end of the age (Matt. 28:20). This is so for one reason: Jesus Christ is divine and not human only. Because he is divine, he can be—and is—omnipresent (present everywhere). Yet, at the same time, because he is human, he cannot be "present everywhere" in his human nature. A human being, by definition, can only be present in one place at one time. A denial of either one of these truths is very damaging to the gospel. The Lutherans, for instance, have taught the doctrine of the ubiquity of the body of Christ. According to this doctrine, since the Ascension the human nature of Christ has actually been present everywhere. Because of this, it is claimed that Christ's physical body and blood are literally present in the sacrament of the Lord's Supper. Now the harm from this is that it contradicts Scripture, which says the heavens must receive Christ until the time of the restoration of all things (Acts 3:2). When the disciples came to the empty tomb of Jesus, the angel said, *"He is not here"* (Luke 24:6). The resurrected body of Christ could not be in more than one place at a time, because it was still a human body. This did not change because of the Ascension. No, said the angel, for *"this same Jesus, who was taken up from you into heaven, will so come in like manner as you saw Him go into heaven"* (Acts 1:11).

The fact that Jesus, in his human nature, is now removed from us is not a disadvantage. To the contrary, as Jesus himself prophesied, it is an advantage. He could not be present everywhere at the same time in his human nature. But once he has gone away from us, with respect to his human nature, he can be with us in another way. This other way is through the person of the Holy Spirit, who, being divine only, and not human, can be present everywhere at the same time. And since our Lord Jesus Christ, in his divine nature, is of one substance with the Holy Spirit, he can be with us through the Spirit. At the same time, as the Catechism reminds us, there is now one who has our nature, who is "in the presence of His Father in heaven." Yes, *"we have an Advocate with the Father, Jesus Christ the righteous"* (1 John 2:1).

It is a staggering thought, but it is actually true: the person in charge of the universe now is human! This is a marvelous guarantee that our future can never be hopeless. And what a glorious thing it is that even though Jesus is absent from us (as to his human nature), he is able to dwell within our hearts by the Holy Spirit whom he sent to be with us—to comfort us and to keep us.

And now, one final note: there is a vast difference between the biblical truth and popular talk about Jesus. Some of this talk that we hear today reduces the Son of God to nothing more than a "little Jesus within." Take for instance the popular chorus that says, "He lives, he lives, Christ Jesus lives today." It ends this way: "You ask me how I know he lives? He lives within my heart." This is not the biblical concept. We know that Jesus lives because God says so in the Bible and because the Holy Spirit (sent by Jesus) attests the truth of the Bible to our hearts. And while there is indeed a sense in which Jesus is living within us, we must never forget that no less important is the fact that our Savior is now absent from us, sitting at the right hand of the Father. The day will come soon when he will return, and every eye will see him. If we forget this, we do not understand the truth of the Ascension.

QUESTIONS ON THE LESSON

1. How is the Ascension sometimes misrepresented today?
2. Why is the charge that the disciples were "prescientific" utterly unconvincing?
3. Is Jesus now present with his people or absent from them?
4. What is wrong with the gospel song that says, "You ask me how I know He lives? He lives within my heart!"
5. What is meant by the doctrine of the ubiquity of the body of Christ? Is this a biblical concept?

QUESTIONS FOR STUDY AND DISCUSSION

1. Why are the absence of Jesus from this earth and his sitting at God's right hand important for the mission of the church? Consider Matthew 28:18–20.
2. Is heaven a place or a state (i.e., a place in the universe or a condition of our existence)? What biblical evidence can you give for your answer?
3. What are the primary works of Christ now as he rules from heaven? What is the goal of all his present work?

LORD'S DAY 19

SCRIPTURE READINGS: *Colossians 1:9–20;*
Ephesians 4:1–16; Matthew 25:31–46

50. **Q. Why is it added, *And sitteth at the right hand of God?***
A. Because Christ ascended into heaven for this end, that He might there appear as Head of His Church, by whom the Father governs all things.

51. **Q. What profit unto us is this glory of Christ, our Head?**
A. First, that by His Holy Spirit He sheds forth heavenly gifts in us, His members; then, that by His power He defends and preserves us against all enemies.

52. **Q. What comfort is it to you that Christ *shall come to judge the living and the dead?***
A. That in all my sorrows and persecutions, with uplifted head I look for the very same Person who before has offered Himself for my sake to the tribunal of God, and has removed all curse from me, to come as Judge from heaven; who shall cast all His and my enemies into everlasting condemnation, but shall take me with all His chosen ones to Himself into heavenly joy and glory.

Christ is seated at the right hand of the Father because his work of atonement is finished. He finished the work that the Father gave him to do here on earth. But he also sits in the place of honor because all authority has been given to him in heaven and on earth (Matt. 28:18–20). It is clear, then, that we must not think of our Lord Jesus as inactive—as one who sits and does nothing. To the contrary, he is just as active today on behalf of his people as he ever was while he was here on earth. He reigns right now over all the universe. He is, right now, bringing about the defeat of all his enemies (1 Cor. 15:24–28). And it is only when this present activity reaches its final goal in the subjection of all things to himself, that our Lord Jesus will return to the earth and—after the final destruction of death itself—deliver it all to the Father.

We do not realize as we should the great things that Jesus is doing for his people. For example, he gives them faithful pastors and teachers (Eph. 4:8–12). He doesn't do this in the same manner that he did when he came to confront Saul of Tarsus on the road to Damascus (Acts 9:1–9). He doesn't appear to men today in his human nature. He now calls men by the power of his written Word—and especially the preached Word—as it is made effective by the power of the Holy Spirit. But it is our Lord Jesus Christ who gives these gifts to the church. And it is Christ who is building the church by his Word and Spirit. But finally, one day, when the whole church of Christ has been gathered in, he will return to this planet.

The return of Christ—often called "the Second Coming"—will not be at all as some people imagine. There are some (modernists) who use the phrase "the Second Coming of Christ" as a symbol. To them it means only that the ideals of Jesus finally triumph, so that the world is "Christianized." "When this ideal state of society comes," they say, "that will be the Second Coming of Jesus." But this is not true. The return of Jesus will be quite literal, as literal as his first coming was nearly two thousand years ago. It will be an awe-inspiring event, plainly visible to people standing on the surface of the earth. They will see Jesus, and—if they are not believers—they will suddenly feel a sickening terror rising within them. They will realize what fools they were to scoff at the warning of these things in the Bible (2 Peter 3). Their hearts will sink as it dawns upon them that it is too late to find his grace and forgiveness.

The Bible says, *"We must all appear before the judgment seat of Christ, that each one may receive the things done in the body, according to what he has done, whether good or bad"* (2 Cor. 5:10). The reason for this is not that there is any uncertainty as to the outcome. The Day of Judgment is not needed in order that God can make up his mind about us. No, the purpose of the Day of Judgment is the public vindication of God's prior decision. He already knows those who belong to him. But on that day all men and angels will also know, and they will see, that God's judgment is just. And the one who will administer this public manifestation of God's justice is none other than our Lord Jesus.

Try to imagine the scene. All men who have ever lived are gathered before the throne of Jesus. There is a public declaration of the eternal destiny of each one. No mouth is opened to object. To the lost it is perfectly clear that they deserve the eternal punishment to which they are consigned. To the saved it is equally clear that they, because of the finished work of Christ, in whom they have put their trust, were made righteous so that there is no sin left to their account for which they ought to be punished.

No one knows just when that great and awesome day will come. As a matter of fact, Jesus himself, when he was on earth, did not know (Mark 3:32). God has not revealed when it will be, so that no one will become complacent. But he has revealed that it will surely come, so that we will all strive to be ready.

The Lord's people are marked out by their conviction that these things are true. They are persuaded of these things not because they are brighter than those who are lost, or because they are more worthy in themselves, or because of anything that they have done to make themselves righteous. No, it is only because they have been united to Jesus Christ, believing in his Word and expecting his return.

And what a difference it makes in everyday living when we do believe! Nowhere in the Bible do we read that the Christian life will be "a bed of roses." To the contrary, in this world—as Jesus said—we will have tribulation (John 16:33). But when we keep our eyes on the great day of Christ and on the great division that is going to come on that day, we count the present adversity as unworthy to be compared with the glory that is coming. May God grant that we may have part with the Lord on that day.

QUESTIONS ON THE LESSON

1. What is Jesus doing right now?
2. What do modernists mean by "the Second Coming"?
3. What does it really mean?
4. Why is the Day of Judgment needed?
5. What is the practical value of believing this doctrine?

QUESTIONS FOR STUDY AND DISCUSSION

1. Discuss various means that Christ presently uses to accomplish his purposes.
2. Is it really possible to believe that Christ rules all things in view of the apparent increase of evil on the earth?
3. Is it Christian to believe that Christ would send men to everlasting punishment? Why do so many who call themselves Christian think otherwise today?

LORD'S DAY 20

SCRIPTURE READINGS: *1 Corinthians 12:1–27;
John 14:16–26; 15:26–16:15; Romans 8:1–17*

53. **Q. What do you believe concerning *the Holy Spirit?***
A. First, that He is true and co-eternal God with the Father
and the Son; second, that He is also given me, to make
me by a true faith partaker of Christ and all His benefits,
to comfort me, and to abide with me forever.

The Heidelberg Catechism is out of step with the times. We say this
because it does not focus attention on the person and work of the Holy
Spirit. A number of Catechism questions and answers are devoted to
the person and work of Christ, but only this one is directly devoted to
the Holy Spirit. In many churches today, this is not so. More and more
the focus is on the Holy Spirit, even more than it is upon the Lord Jesus. However, it is not a bad thing to be out of step with the times—
not when that means being in step with the Word of God. And that is
what the Heidelberg Catechism is.

The Bible itself does not dwell on the person and work of the Holy
Spirit. That is not the focus of Scripture. How could it be, when the
Scripture is inspired by the Holy Spirit? When Jesus was about to leave
the world and go back to the Father, he said that he would not leave his
disciples in this world as *"orphans"* (John 14:18). No, Jesus promised to
send *"another Helper"* (John 14:16), namely, the Holy Spirit. And what
was the principal work that he was to do? Jesus explained, *"He will teach
you all things, and bring to your remembrance all things that I said to you"*
(John 14:26). *"He will not speak on His own authority,"* said Jesus, *"but
whatever He hears He will speak. . . . He will glorify Me"* (John 16:13–14).

Here there is a clear analogy between Christ's work and the Holy Spirit's work. When Christ was on earth, what was his aim? Was it to glorify himself? Was it to draw attention to his own person? The answer is perfectly clear. Christ did not come to be ministered unto, but to minister—and to give his life as a ransom for many. He came, not to do his own will, but to do the will of him who sent him. So he did not glorify himself. He glorified the Father. His entire mission was to humble himself and magnify the Father. And now the Holy Spirit has come, not to glorify himself, but to glorify Jesus.

Now that does not mean that the Holy Spirit is any less worthy of honor than the Father or the Son. No doubt the day will come when the great work of the Holy Spirit—in applying the redemption purchased by Christ—is finished. Then his work will be understood better than it is now. But the Catechism is right—it is biblical—to put the focus on Christ rather than on the Spirit.

The Bible teaches us that the Holy Spirit is God. There is one God, and in the Godhead the Holy Spirit is a person distinct from the Father and the Son. We see this clearly in Matthew 28:19, which says, *"Go therefore and make disciples of all the nations, baptizing them in the name of the Father and of the Son and of the Holy Spirit."* Since our Lord speaks of just one name, there is but one being in relationship to whom men are to be baptized. But since this one name is equally the name *"of the Father and of the Son and of the Holy Spirit,"* there are clearly three persons who equally possess this one divine name. Thus, when Ananias and Sapphira lied to the Holy Spirit (Acts 5:3), the Scripture says they lied to God (Acts 5:4). And to say that we are to be baptized in the name of the one who is the Holy Spirit, is clearly to say that he too is the God of our salvation. We are not saved, in other words, without the great work of the Holy Spirit.

One who understands this will also realize that the whole Catechism is in one sense about the person and work of the Holy Spirit. When we read about faith, for instance (Q/A 21), we learn that it is the Holy Spirit who creates this blessed gift in us. Or again, when we read about the career of our Lord as the Messiah (Q/A 31), we are reminded that it was by the anointing of the Holy Spirit that he was equipped for this threefold office. Or again, to take just one more example, it is the Holy Spirit who teaches us in the holy gospel—and by the sacraments—the meaning of Christ's sacrifice for us (Q/A 67). So the biblical way to see the full glory of the Holy Spirit is to see it—so to speak—indirectly. In other words, we should take note of all the great things that he does to bring us into union with Christ and to a recognition of his glory.

The Catechism simply assumes that the Holy Spirit is given to Christians. This certainly contradicts the popular Pentecostal teaching that the Holy Spirit is given to Christians after they believe in Christ—as an additional or second blessing. Pentecostalism teaches, in other words, a split-level church. On the lower level are the ordinary Christians. They "only" have faith in Jesus, the forgiveness of sin, and everlasting life. But on the higher level are those who have the gift (and gifts) of the Holy Spirit. This is quite unbiblical. The Day of Pentecost was a unique event (Acts 2). It can no more be repeated than can the birth or ascension of Christ. Only once did Jesus Christ send forth—or pour out—his Holy Spirit. Only once did the Holy Spirit come to dwell in Christ's body, the church. And if we belong to Christ, we are members of his body. This is because we already have the Holy Spirit (1 Cor. 12:13). If we did not have the Spirit, we would not belong to Christ.

QUESTIONS ON THE LESSON

1. In what way is the Heidelberg Catechism out of step with the times?
2. Is this to the detriment of the Catechism? Why?
3. In what way is the present work of the Spirit like the work that Jesus did when he was on earth?
4. In what sense can it be said that the whole Catechism is about the person and work of the Holy Spirit?
5. What is the fundamental error of Pentecostalism?

QUESTIONS FOR STUDY AND DISCUSSION

1. Discuss the following proposition: The stress of Pentecostalism upon the work of the Holy Spirit leads to extreme subjectivism in religion. It tends to deemphasize doctrine and the objective work of Christ.
2. Is it possible to prove that someone's reported experiences are of the Holy Spirit? Can these be distinguished from merely psychological experiences? Does the rest of such a person's life have any bearing on the interpretation you give to his reported experiences?

3. Since the Holy Spirit works repentance and faith in us, should we look for some inner experience as an assurance of our salvation?
4. Can the experience of a miracle (e.g., speaking in tongues or miraculous healing) give us assurance of salvation? Do you think this is why so many people seek such miraculous experiences?

LORD'S DAY 21

SCRIPTURE READINGS: *Matthew 16:13–28;*
Ephesians 2:11–22; Acts 20:17–32

54. **Q. What do you believe concerning the *holy catholic*
Church?**

A. That the Son of God, out of the whole human race, from
the beginning to the end of the world, gathers, defends,
and preserves for Himself, by His Spirit and Word, in the
unity of the true faith, a Church chosen to everlasting life;
and that I am, and forever shall remain, a living member
thereof.

It was a critical moment in the ministry of Christ. The big crowds were
leaving. The opposition was increasing. His enemies were plotting his
downfall. The time had come for his disciples to stand up and be
counted. Jesus therefore asked them, *"Who do men say that I, the Son of
Man, am?"* (Matt. 16:13). They answered that people had a variety of
opinions. "But what about you?" asked Jesus. Peter answered rightly:
"You are the Christ, the Son of the living God" (v. 16). Peter did not come
to that conclusion because he was so brilliant, but because God had
been pleased to reveal it to him (v. 17). Then Jesus went on to speak
about the church. He said that he would build his church on *"this rock"*
(v. 18) and that the gates of hell would not prevail against it.

Bible commentators have long disagreed as to the exact meaning
of *"this rock."* Was it Peter himself? Or was it Peter's confession? In our
view, it was the two together! The church was founded upon Peter believing in Jesus as the Messiah of God. This must be the meaning, because Paul says, *"No other foundation can anyone lay than that which is*

laid, which is Jesus Christ" (1 Cor. 3:11). At the same time, the church has been "built on the foundation of the apostles and prophets, Jesus Christ Himself being the chief cornerstone" (Eph. 2:20). These statements are in perfect agreement in the light of Peter's inspired comment that we also "as living stones, are being built up a spiritual house" by "coming to" the Lord Jesus (1 Peter 2:4–5).

Christ presently builds his church through the power of his Holy Spirit and through the truth of his word in the Scriptures. Those who come to believe in him become living stones, just as Peter himself did at the beginning. But what kind of church is this that Jesus is building? The first thing we should note is that Jesus is the one who is building this church. We must never lose sight of this in the midst of the many distressing divisions that we see. This does not mean that we should forget about everything else and make visible unity the only principle that guides our actions. No, the church is also described in the Bible as holy. This reminds us that faithfulness to Christ and to the holy Scriptures is also essential. We must also realize that the true church of Christ is "catholic" or "universal." This means that it will always transcend the culture of any nation. The church must therefore resist conformity to the spirit of any culture or era.

The true church—in all ages and places—has one faith that unites it, despite its outward divisions. What Christians believed in the first century is the same in all essential points as what Christians still believe today. And right here we see how important it is for the church to be creedal. The great salvation given by God—revealed to us in the Scriptures—is exactly the same as it was when it was first given nearly two thousand years ago. That is why Christians today still confess their faith in the words of the Apostles' Creed. The great work of Jesus Christ is historical in nature and therefore immune to the least alteration.

There is, however, an important distinction in the unfolding of the plan of salvation. It was not made clear in the Old Testament Scriptures just how the whole human race would partake of Abraham's blessing. During the period of time beginning with Abraham, the church was confined to one nation. The older situation, in which at least some men out there in the wider world still knew the true God (think of Melchizedek), died out. After this, for about two thousand years, the members of the church were mostly people out of the Israelite nation. There were always a few outsiders brought into Israel, like Rahab and Ruth, to remind the covenant people that they were not the only heirs of salvation. But the middle wall of partition between Jew and Gentile was broken down only when Christ finally came.

Now the way has been opened up for the Gentiles to belong to the true Israel of God on an equal basis with Jews. As a matter of fact, the tables are now exactly reversed. The Jews are now mostly excluded— because of their own prejudice. Yet all the way through the Old and New Testament eras alike, it has only been by the sovereign work of the Holy Spirit that any Jews or Gentiles have been made willing to receive the Messiah. And the day will yet come when the Jews will return to the Messiah en masse. But even then the church will be one—not di-vided between Jews and Gentiles—because all who truly believe in Christ are living stones in the same building.

The final point that the Catechism makes is that we must be sure we belong to this body of redeemed people. And the only way that we can do that is to be sure we belong to Jesus. If we sincerely believe in him and obey him as Lord, then the same thing will be true of us that was true of Peter. It was not flesh and blood that brought us to this, but the power and grace of our heavenly Father.

QUESTIONS ON THE LESSON

1. What did Jesus mean by *"this rock"*?
2. What texts prove this?
3. What are some of the characteristics of the church that Christ is building?
4. Why is a faithful church a creedal church?
5. In what way is the church today different from the church under the Old Testament?
6. In what way is it the same?

QUESTIONS FOR STUDY AND DISCUSSION

1. What value do creeds have today in this age of anti-intellectualism and anticreedalism?
2. Is the church a mystical, invisible body to which we belong regard-less of any actual connection with a particular congregation? What Scripture would you give to support your answer?

3. Some say that the church began on the Day of Pentecost. What reasons would you give to support the statement of the Catechism that the church has been gathered, defended, and preserved "from the beginning to the end of the world"?
4. This view of the church as an historical body is one not many Christians have been taught. Why is it important to view the church historically?

LORD'S DAY 21—CONTINUED

SCRIPTURE READINGS: *Acts 8:4–24; 1 Corinthians 12:12–27; 1 Peter 1*

55. **Q. What do you understand by** *the communion of saints?*
A. First, that believers, all and every one, as members of Christ, are partakers of Him and of all His treasures and gifts; second, that every one must know himself bound to employ his gifts readily and cheerfully for the advantage and salvation of other members.

56. **Q. What do you believe concerning** *the forgiveness of sins?*
A. That God, for the sake of Christ's satisfaction, will no more remember my sins, neither my sinful nature, against which I have to struggle all my life long; but will graciously grant unto me the righteousness of Christ, that I may never come into condemnation.

Did you ever notice what happens when a congregation recites the Apostles' Creed? There is usually a pause between the phrases "the holy catholic church" and "the communion of saints," as if these two things were quite distinct from each other. But, in fact, "the holy catholic church" *is* "the communion of saints." You might say that the second phrase gives us a definition of the first. When we understand that the church is the communion of saints, we also understand what is meant by "the holy catholic church."

For some people, the first phrase is a real problem. The only use of the word *catholic* that they know is in the name of a particular de-nomination, namely, the Roman Catholic Church. They do not want to be identified with that denomination, so they find it difficult to re-cite this part of the creed. What they need to understand is that the word *catholic* simply means "universal." It refers to the one true church of God, extending down through the ages (and including that part which existed long before Rome ever came into the picture). This church began soon after the fall of man. It is our view that when God first promised to send a Savior, there was a believing response. The way in which Eve named her son (see Gen. 4:1) suggests that she was a be-liever. We know for sure, in any event, that Abel was a believer (Heb. 11:4). What we see, then, down through the whole history of man, is that God has been gathering out of the lost human race those whom he makes holy. These people constitute a communion of saints, because the word *saint* in the Bible simply means "holy one." They were not holy originally. They were, by nature, no different from the others (Eph. 2:3). But because God chose them and through his Holy Spirit—and by his Word—gave them the ability to repent of their sins and believe in him, they became members of the body of Christ, a community of people made holy. And every person who truly repents and believes in Christ is a part of this body of people. This is what we have in mind when we speak of a holy catholic church. It is not something that we can see with our eyes. It can only be "seen" by the eye of faith! Yet it really exists—this one, holy fellowship of genuine Christians.

When we think of the church as we see it in a local congregation of people who profess to believe in Jesus, we must acknowledge that we see many things that distress us. As a matter of fact, this sometimes be-comes such a big problem that people give up on "the visible church" completely and claim to belong only to "the invisible church"—that is, the holy catholic church, the communion of saints! It is even possible for people to hold this view in the vain imagination that this makes them more saintly than others. Yet the truth is that this is a serious er-ror. This is quite clear from the Scripture. Take, for instance, the Great Commission (Matt. 28:18–20). When Jesus gave that command to his church, it involved definite visible actions (such as baptizing and teach-ing). It is also clear, from the pages of the New Testament, that the apostolic church was a highly visible entity. People constantly met to-gether and shared what they had with each other (Acts 2:44–47). And when people were baptized, *"the Lord added"* them to the visible body of believers (v. 47). So the only way one could become a member of the so-called "invisible church" was by joining the church that was visible! No doubt that is one reason why Jesus gave sacraments to the church. They were not invisible sacraments, because the church itself was not meant to be invisible!

However, it is true that there is what we might call a discrepancy between the lines of demarcation. That is, there will always be some in the visible church who are not living in union with Christ. We think, here, of one such as Judas. He did have a place in the Apostolate, and yet he did not have union with Jesus. We know there will always be tares mixed in with the wheat in the visible church.

This raises two important questions. First, how can I know whether the people in a particular congregation are a part of the holy catholic church, the communion of the saints? The answer is that I can know this if there is no doubt about their faithful witness for Jesus. A true church is a church where the true gospel is faithfully preached and where the people are in observable submission to Jesus. Where that is not the case—or, in other words, where error prevails—there is no basis for such assurance.

Second, how can I be sure that I myself have a saving union with Jesus? The answer is that I can be sure if I believe in Christ for my salvation and yield willing obedience to what he commands me. The Bible says that God made Jesus to be sin for us, that we might—in him—be made righteous (2 Cor. 5:21). What this means is that the believer's sin is "laid to the account of Jesus," while his perfect righteousness is imputed to them! If I really believe in the atonement of Christ, then there is no way that I will refuse what he commands me.

We see, then, that there is a close connection among these three questions and answers of the Catechism. This is because the foundation of the holy catholic church is our Savior's atonement. All of those who are under the blood are his redeemed people. And all of those who are not do not really belong to him—not even if they belong to one of the purest visible churches.

There is one other thing that we should mention before we leave this part of the Catechism. It is the fact that there is no legitimate place for individualism in the life of the believer. This is one of our great problems today. Too many "members" think of the church only in terms of what it gives them, rather than in terms of what they can give others. But the Bible says that we are all members of one another, that we all need the gifts that others have, and that we have something that we ought to give to others. What this means is that if we are not faithfully participating in the life of a faithful local church, we are not really living as Christians. Let us say, for instance, that you do not bother to come to church on Sunday evening. You say, "Well, I just don't feel that I need it!" Your problem is that you are thinking of the church only in terms of what you get from it. You ought to think as well of what you can give to others. The truth is that when you are not there, the body— as a whole—is weakened. This is true because the holy catholic church is a holy communion of believers.

QUESTIONS ON THE LESSON

1. What does the word *catholic* mean in the creed?
2. When did the holy catholic church begin?
3. Who belongs to the catholic church?
4. Can a person belong to "the invisible church" without belonging to a faithful visible church?
5. What does the case of Judas prove?
6. How can one be sure that a particular church is a true one?
7. How can I be sure that I belong to the body of Christ?
8. What is individualism and what is wrong with it?

QUESTIONS FOR STUDY AND DISCUSSION

1. What weaknesses become increasingly evident in the lives of people who claim to be Christians and yet refuse to join a faithful church?
2. In what ways are members of the church supposed to serve and enrich the other members? Is this attitude of serving characteristic of your Christian life? Is it characteristic of others in your church?

LORD'S DAY 22

SCRIPTURE READINGS: *1 Corinthians 15:12–19;*
2 Corinthians 5:18; Philippians 1:21–24

57. **Q.** **What comfort does *the resurrection of the body* afford you?**

A. That not only my soul, after this life, shall immediately be taken up to Christ, its Head; but also that this my body, raised by the power of Christ, shall again be united with my soul, and made like unto the glorious body of Christ.

58. **Q.** **What comfort do you derive from the article of *the life everlasting?***

A. That, since I now feel in my heart the beginning of eternal joy, after this life I shall possess perfect bliss, such as eye has not seen nor ear heard, neither has entered into the heart of man—therein to praise God forever.

It is interesting—but sometimes a bit of a shock—to discover what some people mean when they speak of "the resurrection of the body." Some years ago, I met a woman who was considered to be quite evangelical. She professed to believe the whole Bible. But she did not really understand this vital doctrine. She was about to undergo a serious heart operation. I went to visit her, to encourage and pray with her. I prayed that the Lord would grant success in the operation and healing to her body. She expressed appreciation for my visit, but she also said something like this: "Well, it doesn't matter much about this old body anyway, because one of these days I will be through with it forever."

As soon as I heard that statement, I began to wonder what she meant. I discussed it with her, and it turned out that she did not believe that dead bodies that are laid in the grave will ever arise and live again. This was a shock to me. And, by the way, in the end it was a big shock to her as well. You see, this woman had belonged to a church that was not preaching the gospel faithfully. Without realizing it, she had been influenced by false teaching to the extent that she did not believe in the bodily resurrection. And yet, as soon as I asked her what happened to the body of Jesus, she said, "Why, of course, he got up again and walked out the grave." As soon as it was pointed out that we are to be like him, she realized her error.

Yes, the Bible teaches that Christ is the firstfruits of those who have "slept." What happened to him will happen to us. He was killed and buried, but then, on the third day after that, he was made alive again in *the same body*. Now of course his body was changed—changed by way of *glorification*. But it was still the same in identity (as one could see by the scars from the wounds he had suffered when he was dying). We could perhaps illustrate this—and, we hope, without any sense of irreverence—in the following manner. A certain man had an old Model T Ford. It was rusting and falling to pieces. So he took it all to a foundry and said, "Melt it down and make me a new model." And so they melted down that old car and made a brand new car out of that molten metal. Now was the new car the same car as the old one, or was it a different car? The answer, of course, is that it was both. It was the same car in one sense, a different car in another. The car was the same in substance but different in power and glory. And so it is with the old body made new by the resurrection. The clearest analogy is the one suggested by Q/A 58 of the Catechism.

There is comfort in this doctrine of the resurrection of the body, because eternal life is already a present possession. It is what John had in mind when he spoke of *"the first resurrection"* (Rev. 20:5–6). The Bible says that *"the natural man"* (1 Cor. 2:14)—the unsaved man, who does not have the Holy Spirit—is already dead (Eph. 2:1, 5), even though he does not know it. Death is not, as is commonly thought, only something that looms as a future danger. No, death is something that already holds the natural man in its grip. It is certainly true that the separation of the body and soul is a part of this terrible enemy called death, but it is only one aspect. The essence of death is separation from God and his favor. Well, when the Holy Spirit comes into our hearts, we are made alive again by his power. And this wonderful experience (which has various biblical names, such as regeneration and the new birth) is *the first resurrection.*"

Well, if I really have this new life in me, then I already have the first installment (as it were) of the resurrection glory promised by God. If I have already experienced the first resurrection, then I can have assurance that I will experience the second one, too. Or, to use the language of the Catechism itself, "Since I now feel in my heart [the one], after this life I shall possess [the other]." The reason for this is simply that they are two parts of one process.

We realize, of course, that there are some big problems with this teaching. There always seems to be the question, How is such a thing possible? What about people who have been eaten by animals or who have been burned up in fires? How can such bodies be resurrected? The answer to this is that we simply do not know how life was restored to the body of Jesus. But if God says it will certainly be, then why should we doubt that he has the needed power and wisdom? Is it not true that God has worked great signs and wonders again and again? And is it not true, in our own experience as believers, that he has made us alive again in the Lord Jesus? Is it any harder to change a dead body than it is to change the dead heart of a sinner? No, the Bible says that both of these things require the sovereign and wonder-working power of Jehovah.

If a man understands what has happened to him when he is made a new creature, he will not find it too much to believe in the resurrection of the body. For, while it is true (as the Catechism says) that God has promised "perfect bliss, such as eye has not seen nor ear heard, neither has entered into the heart of man," it is also true that these things are revealed to us by his Spirit (1 Cor. 2:10).

QUESTIONS ON THE LESSON

1. Why did the woman mentioned at the beginning of the lesson really not believe in the resurrection of the body?
2. How was she convinced that believers would actually be raised bodily from the dead?
3. Is the resurrected body the same as the body put in the grave?
4. What are the two aspects of resurrection? What are the two aspects of death?

5. Which is harder: to change the heart of a sinner or to raise a dead body?

QUESTIONS FOR STUDY AND DISCUSSION

1. Give scriptural proof that when we die we are consciously in the presence of Christ.
2. What reasons do liberal Christians give for not believing in the resurrection of the body?
3. What correspondence can be seen between our creation and our resurrection?
4. Will you be able to recognize people you know in their resurrected bodies?

Lord's Day 23

Scripture readings: *Romans 3:19–26; 6; 7; John 1:1–18*

59. Q. But what does it profit you now that you believe all this?

A. That I am righteous in Christ before God, and an heir to eternal life.

60. Q. How are you righteous before God?

A. Only by a true faith in Jesus Christ; that is, though my conscience accuse me that I have grievously sinned against all the commandments of God and kept none of them, and am still inclined to all evil, yet God, without any merit of mine, of mere grace, grants and imputes to me the perfect satisfaction, righteousness, and holiness of Christ, as if I had never had nor committed any sin, and myself had accomplished all the obedience which Christ has rendered for me; if only I accept such benefit with a believing heart.

61. Q. Why do you say that you are righteous only by faith?

A. Not that I am acceptable to God on account of the worthiness of my faith, but because only the satisfaction, righteousness, and holiness of Christ is my righteousness before God, and I can receive the same and make it my own in no other way than by faith only.

In the previous thirty-two Catechism questions and answers, we have been considering the Apostles' Creed. At this point we reach a certain conclusion. If we really believe all these things that are taught in the

Creed, what difference does it make? The answer is that it makes a very big difference, because one who truly believes these things has a "true faith" in the Lord Jesus, and whoever has that is justified and accepted by God as righteous.

Now this doesn't mean that faith itself is a kind of work that has merit. As a matter of fact, the right way to think about faith is in exactly the opposite direction. When you realize, as the Catechism says, that you have "grievously sinned against all the commandments of God," and that even now you are "still inclined to all evil," the last thought that would ever enter your mind is that your faith could merit salvation. No, the very thing that brought you to believe in the first place was your realization that there was no way that you could ever hope to have salvation by your own merit. Faith is not a meritorious work whereby we ourselves do something to earn God's favor. No, true faith is rather a looking entirely away from ourselves to another who merits salvation for us. When you see that there is only one possible source from which you can be right with God—the perfect work of the Lord Jesus—then you look to him as your righteousness. In this manner you are right with God.

Faith itself is not the source of our righteousness. The source is exclusively Jesus. He lived a sinless life and was therefore well pleasing to the heavenly Father. Jesus was also willing to give that righteousness to us. Not only that, but he was willing to bear our sin, our guilt, and our punishment as our substitute. On the basis of this double imputation (of his righteousness to us, and our sin to him), he was condemned and we are put right with God. What puts faith in the spotlight, as it were, is the fact that it is by faith alone that we receive this righteousness. Just as it is by a living eye (not a glass eye) that we can see (receive) the light of a beautiful sunset, so it is by a genuine faith (not a dead faith, as James says) that we receive the righteousness of the Lord Jesus. There is no other way that we can receive the righteousness of Christ. We receive it only by relying on him completely.

It should be obvious that when we say "by faith only," we do not mean "faith in isolation." Here again, it may help us to think of the seeing eye in order to understand this. It is by the eye alone that we can see things. But there never was an eye that could see in isolation. If you ever see a human eye lying on a slab in a laboratory, you can be sure that that eye sees nothing. The reason is that an eye functions only as a living part of a human body. So it is with faith. If you have "faith" all by itself—faith in isolation—then your faith is dead rather than living (James 2:26). In other words, genuine faith in the Lord Jesus will be accompanied by a repentant heart and a willingness to obey his commandments. Nonetheless, it is by faith alone that I am righteous. All I need to do is accept the gift of God by faith in order to become right with God.

There is one other thing that we must correctly understand in this section. It is the statement, "I . . . am still inclined to all evil." This does not mean that all that we do is sin, that there is nothing good in us. No, this clause should be taken in parallel with the preceding clauses as an accusation of our consciences ("though my conscience accuse me that I have grievously sinned against all the commandments of God and kept none of them, and am still inclined to all evil"). There are two testimonies that we hear: our consciences and the Word of God. Our consciences still accuse us of our sin and our inclination to all kinds of sin. But a greater testimony comes from God, and he declares that we are right with him through faith in Christ. Both testimonies are true, but the testimony of God concerns our standing in his sight, while the testimony of our consciences concerns our condition, which is yet far from perfect.

A great change takes place in us when we believe in Jesus as our Savior—when God declares us righteous in his sight. This is perfectly clear in the Bible. When Paul says, *"I know that in me (that is, in my flesh) nothing good dwells"* (Rom. 7:18), he doesn't mean that this gives the whole picture. No, if one thing is clear—in this entire chapter—it is that there is a conflict within the apostle. There is the old nature (he is still inclined to sin), but there is also the new nature (he now delights in God's holy commandments) (Rom. 7:22). And if this is true, it is not adequate for a new creature in Christ to say simply, "I am still inclined to all evil." It is certainly true that there is still a law of sin in our members. Yet, at the same time, the new man delights in the law of God because he has a new nature! So we must be careful that we do not make a wrong use of what is stated in Answer 60.

Whenever a Christian looks at himself, however, one thing is perfectly certain. He is not going to see anything there that will make him think he has made himself righteous. He differs in a radical way from the unbeliever. But the main difference is that he looks completely away from himself and to the Lord Jesus for the whole of his salvation.

QUESTIONS ON THE LESSON

1. From what must faith be carefully distinguished?
2. What is meant by "double imputation"?
3. What is meant by saying, "We are saved by faith alone, but not by a faith that is alone"?
4. How does the illustration of the eye help us understand this?
5. Prove from Scripture that the Catechism statement "I . . . am still inclined to all evil" is, in and of itself, far from being the whole truth about a true believer.

QUESTIONS FOR STUDY AND DISCUSSION

1. Discuss the following: We are saved by works; without perfect works no one can be saved.
2. How can we be right with God and still sin? Justification is God's declaration that because of the perfect work of Christ we are, through faith in him, righteous in the sight of God. How can God make such a declaration while we still commit sin?
3. Are there various kinds of faith? Two were mentioned in the lesson— (1) living faith, which saves, and (2) dead faith, which does not save. Discuss how these manifest themselves.

LORD'S DAY 24

SCRIPTURE READINGS: *Psalm 14; Matthew 6:1–18;*
7:15–27; 25:31–46; Philippians 3:1–16

62. **Q. But why cannot our good works be the whole or part of
our righteousness before God?**

A. Because the righteousness which can stand before the tribunal of God must be absolutely perfect and wholly con-
formable to the divine law, while even our best works in
this life are all imperfect and defiled with sin.

63. **Q. What? Do our good works then merit nothing, while
God will yet reward them in this and in the future life?**

A. This reward is not of merit but of grace.

64. **Q. But does not this doctrine make men careless and profane?**

A. By no means; for it is impossible that those who are im-
planted into Christ by a true faith should not bring forth
fruits of thankfulness.

God is love. The Bible says so (1 John 4:8). But that is not all that it says.
It also says that God is light, and that in him there is no darkness at all (1
John 1:5). The great problem in much of what is called "church" today is
that it has had too much unbalanced teaching. It has emphasized love to
such an extent that God's absolute holiness has been compromised, if not
forgotten. Yet the fact is that the true and living God never has compromised with evil and never will compromise with it in any way. Therefore,
the only righteousness that counts with him at all is perfect righteousness.

Now to people today this sounds very strange, because (as we say) "nobody is perfect." And since nobody is perfect, it seems as if God is unfair to expect us to be. What people fail to understand is the momentous fact that man was created by God in his own image and endowed by him with ability to live perfectly. If God had made us the way we are now and then condemned us for being that way, it would have been unjust. But there is no injustice when God requires us to live up to the potential with which we were created.

The trouble is that we no longer have the original potential. We lost it forever when we all sinned in Adam's transgression. It follows, then, that nothing can satisfy God's absolute standards, except for the righteousness of the Lord Jesus. If we imagine that we can do anything even to help establish our righteousness in God's sight, we misunderstand what God requires. He requires perfection. And perfection is like a seamless garment. Even if I could begin today to live a sinless life, I still could never meet God's absolute standard because of the sin I have already committed. And, of course, we all know only too well that we have not managed to live perfectly for even one single day. So the very idea of a self-produced righteousness is utterly abhorred and renounced by every true believer.

Yet, in spite of the fact that our very best is far from the perfection that God demands, he will reward the "good works" of his people. As a matter of fact, the one great criterion of judgment will be good works. God will see them in his people and not see them in those who are cast into the lake of fire with Satan and his angels (Matt. 25:31–46). But why does God reward his people for the imperfect good they do? The answer is that it pleases him to do so. It is his good pleasure to do it as an undeserved favor. A human father will sometimes reward his son for something he has done, even though the work he did is substandard. (Think of a son's first attempt to make a gift for his dad out of clay or wood.) What he rewards is really the loving intention that he sees in his son rather than the imperfect product. Yet the product is the infallible proof that there was this loving intention. It is something like this with the rewards that God will give to his people on the Day of Judgment. While their good works will not merit a reward, they will be an infallible indication of the faith that motivated them.

Will anyone be saved in spite of having no good works for God to reward on the Day of Judgment? The answer is no, it is not possible to be united to Christ and at the same time to be entirely devoid of the good works that result from that union. I once knew a man who had an apple orchard. He would graft branches of one type onto a tree of a different species. Sometimes the graft would not take, and the branch would wither and die because the life-sustaining sap did not flow through it. But whenever that life-sustaining sap did flow through that branch, you would know it by the fruit it produced.

It is like that with those who believe. Those who have true faith are united with Jesus and produce the fruit of that union. There is no such thing as union with him that does not produce good fruit. Even the thief who died on the cross beside Jesus began—as soon as he trusted in Christ—to bear witness to the unbeliever. The fruit was there as soon as he had living union with Jesus. So it is with all who are brought into Christ as real believers.

Here is a way to test our understanding. Notice two interesting things that our Lord Jesus says about the Day of Judgment. On the one hand, he says that when he begins to praise the saved for the good works they did, they will be amazed. They will ask, "When did we see You hungry and feed You, or thirsty and give You drink?" (Matt. 25:37). But when he deals with the lost, it will be very different. They will say, "Lord, Lord, have we not prophesied in Your name, cast out demons in Your name, and done many wonders in Your name?" (Matt. 7:22). They have a list (you could say) of the "good works" they did. Yet to them Jesus will solemnly say, "Depart from Me, you who practice lawlessness!" (Matt. 7:23). Now precisely what is the difference? It is that the ungodly look upon their best works as having merit. For this very reason they are perfectly obnoxious to the Lord Jesus. The godly, on the other hand, see nothing meritorious in their own works. On the contrary, their hope is built on the righteousness and sacrifice of the Lord Jesus alone. For this very reason, the good works they do are pleasing to God. In their case it is Jesus himself who is pleased to keep the record and to reward them on the Day of Judgment. The only good works that can ever please God are the ones that we do with no thought whatever of merit.

QUESTIONS ON THE LESSON

1. In what way has there been a lack of balance in the teaching of much of the visible church?
2. What has resulted from this lack of balance?

3. Why is it not unfair for God to demand perfection, even though we are no longer capable of it?
4. Why does Scripture speak of our works as the criterion for God's judgment on the Last Day?
5. Can a man be saved if he has no good works?
6. How do the saved and the lost differ in their attitudes toward their own works?

QUESTIONS FOR STUDY AND DISCUSSION

1. Should believers work for a reward in heaven? What light does Matthew 6:19–21 shed on this matter?
2. If being united to Christ always produces good works in the believer, why do some who make a profession of faith show no fruit? And why are some Christians finally put out of the church (excommunicated)?
3. We said a man cannot be saved without good works. What amount of good works must the believer have to be saved?
4. What does the subject of this lesson imply about modern funeral practices? (Hint: How does one get into heaven according to modern ideas?)

Lord's Day 25

SCRIPTURE READINGS: *Romans 10:17;*
1 Corinthians 1:26–32; Genesis 17:1–14; Colossians 2:11–12

65. **Q. Since, then, we are made partakers of Christ and all His benefits by faith only, whence comes this faith?**

A. From the Holy Spirit, who works it in our hearts by the preaching of the holy gospel, and confirms it by the use of the holy sacraments.

66. **Q. What are the sacraments?**

A. The sacraments are holy, visible signs and seals, appointed of God for this end, that by the use thereof He may the more fully declare and seal to us the promise of the gospel; namely, that He of grace grants us the remission of sins and life eternal, for the sake of the one sacrifice of Christ accomplished on the cross.

67. **Q. Are, then, both the Word and the sacraments designed to direct our faith to the sacrifice of Jesus Christ on the cross as the only ground of our salvation?**

A. Yes, indeed; for the Holy Spirit teaches us in the gospel and assures us by the sacraments that the whole of our salvation stands in the one sacrifice of Christ made for us on the cross.

68. **Q. How many sacraments has Christ instituted in the new covenant or testament?**

A. Two: holy baptism and the holy supper.

If the gospel is to be faithfully preached, it must be preached to all without distinction. We know from the Scriptures, of course, that some are elect while others are not. But God has not told us who is elect and who is not. What he has told us is that we are to preach the gospel—which means "good news"—to all men everywhere. And it really *is* good news. The good news is that Christ died for sinners, and that all who repent and believe will have eternal life. Why is it, then, that some who hear the good news believe while others refuse to do so? Well, the answer to that question will have to be found in one of two places. We will have to find the ultimate reason either in man himself or in the sovereign work of the Holy Spirit.

Many people want to find the ultimate reason in man. They say, "This man (we will call him Mr. Grey) came to Jesus because there was at least a small element of goodness in him that was not in Mr. Brown." Or, to put it negatively, "Mr. Brown did not have faith because he did something wicked. He resisted the Spirit, while Mr. Grey was not quite that bad; he gave up his resisting." The trouble with this concept is that the Bible says there is no difference between us. We are all dead in our transgressions. That is our natural condition. Therefore, the above scenario lacks a factual basis.

We learn from God's Word that he begins the good work in us (Phil. 1:6). Then, after he begins it, we repent of our sins and believe in Christ as our only Savior. In the words of Jesus, "*It is the Spirit who gives life; the flesh profits nothing*" (John 6:63). So, it is not only the Word preached that causes faith to exist in God's people. No, it is the Word preached together with the regenerating work of the Holy Spirit. Here a simple illustration will help us to see the connection. Imagine a man who sits in pitch darkness. He sits in complete darkness for two reasons. In the first place, there is no light. In the second place, his eyes are blinded. What does he need, then, in order to see? He needs two "gifts" to be given to him by someone else. He needs someone to turn on the light and then someone to restore his eyesight. The preaching of the Word of God is like turning on the light. Everyone who hears the Word is exposed to the light. Regeneration (making the dead man alive again) is like restoring the man's eyesight. Regeneration restores one's ability to understand spiritual things. Both preaching and regeneration are essential. We see, then, that the ultimate answer is found not in man himself but in the sovereign work of the Holy Spirit. The Holy Spirit regenerates those whom God has elected. And because he makes them alive from the dead, they are able to respond to the gospel offer.

The sacraments, for many believers, present a problem. The reason for this—as we see it—is that they do not understand their nature or function. A fine Christian once said me, "I just don't seem to get anything out of the Lord's Supper. It just doesn't do anything to me— I seem to get more out of preaching." His problem was that he expected something from the sacrament quite different from what he received through preaching. But there is only one gospel, and it comes to us both by preaching and by the sacraments. We can see this clearly if we simply recall that the sacraments are signs and seals (Rom. 4:11).

Let us try to illustrate. Consider such a simple thing as a warm handshake, as a sign of real friendship. If you are my friend, and I haven't seen you for a long time, you will surely give me a warm handshake. But the handshake itself is not what binds us together. No, what binds us together is our esteem—yes, our love—for each other. But still, the handshake *does* count. It *is* important. The warm way that we shake hands shows that our friendship is solid. The handshake is a sign of the reality of the friendship—but (and this is the important thing) the friendship was already there before our handshake could be a sign of it.

Again, consider my diploma. It shows that I am a bona fide graduate of a theological seminary. You are assured of it because it bears the seal of the institution that issued it. The authorities affixed the seal to attest what the diploma says. But, obviously, the seal itself did not prepare me as a preacher. No, it was the long hours of hard work, under the faculty's teaching. I had to have *that* before I could have the seal that attests it.

Why is it, then, that my friend did not "feel" anything more in the sacrament than he "felt" in the preaching? Well, the answer is quite simple: there was nothing there that was different. The "feeling" in the handshake is not different from the "feeling" that is already there in the friendship—it is the same. The message of the seal on my diploma is not different from the message on the diploma itself—it is the same. This doesn't mean that signs and seals add nothing. They do add something. The handshake adds something because it confirms the warmth of our friendship. The seal adds something to the diploma because it confirms the authority of its declaration. And so it is with the holy sacraments. They do add something to gospel preaching. They add an element of assurance to the message we hear in the preaching. Just as I feel my friend's handshake and say to myself, "Yes, he really is my friend," so also in the sacraments I receive reassurance from Jesus. He reassures me that I really am saved by the self-sacrifice he made for me.

The Church of Rome says there are seven sacraments, but we only find two in the Scriptures. Only God can institute a sacrament. Men have no right to institute sacraments without a command from the Lord Jesus. And the only sacraments he has commanded are baptism and the Lord's Supper. We will touch upon this at a later time, but here it ought to be mentioned that God determines how we are to worship him. That which is not commanded is therefore forbidden. If God himself does not say in his Word, "Do this as a sign and seal of the covenant of salvation," then we must say, "It is forbidden." The Church of Rome has added five ceremonies, which it calls sacraments, to the two that Christ commanded. However, since these were not commanded by God, they are *therefore* forbidden. It is a sad fact, however, that this principle is widely neglected today. It is even rejected in some Reformed churches. But we will return to this matter later.

QUESTIONS ON THE LESSON

1. Why should the gospel be preached to all men, if only some men are elect?
2. Why do some respond to the gospel, while others do not?
3. How does the illustration of a blind man sitting in the dark help us to understand what is needed by those who are outside of Christ?
4. Is there anything in the sacraments that is not in the gospel? Explain.
5. Why do we, as Reformed Christians, reject five of the seven sacraments taught by the Roman Catholic Church?

QUESTIONS FOR STUDY AND DISCUSSION

1. Discuss the similarities and differences between the New Testament sacraments, baptism and the Lord's Supper, and the Old Testament sacraments, circumcision and the Passover.
2. Many Christians have the idea that we are born again as a result of our decision to accept Christ. What is wrong with this idea?

3. If the sacraments add nothing new to gospel preaching, then why do we need to observe them at all?
4. For what reasons should marriage not be considered a sacrament?

Lord's Day 26

SCRIPTURE READINGS: *Romans 6:1–7; 1 Peter 3:18–22; Acts 2:38–39; Matthew 28:18–20*

69. Q. How is it signified and sealed unto you in holy baptism that you have part in the one sacrifice of Christ on the cross?

A. Thus, that Christ has appointed this outward washing with water and added the promise that I am washed with His blood and Spirit from the pollution of my soul, that is, from all my sins, as certainly as I am washed outwardly with water, by which the filthiness of the body is commonly washed away.

70. Q. What is it to be washed with the blood and Spirit of Christ?

A. It is to have the forgiveness of sins from God through grace, for the sake of Christ's blood, which He shed for us in His sacrifice on the cross; and also to be renewed by the Holy Spirit, and sanctified to be members of Christ, that so we may more and more die unto sin and lead holy and unblamable lives.

71. Q. Where has Christ assured us that we are washed with His blood and Spirit as certainly as we are washed with the water of baptism?

A. In the institution of baptism, which reads thus: *Go ye therefore, and make disciples of all the nations, baptizing them into the name of the Father and of the Son and of the Holy Spirit,*

> Matt. 28:19. And: *He that believeth and is baptized shall be saved; but he that disbelieveth shall be condemned,* Mark 16:16. This promise is also repeated where the Scripture calls baptism *the washing of regeneration* and *the washing away of sins,* Tit. 3:5; Acts 22:16.

If baptism were only a humanly devised symbol, it could hardly bring us assurance. But it was, in fact, instituted by the Lord Jesus. That makes all the difference. Here, once again, we will try to illustrate. If I desire friendship with you, and in order to assure myself that you are my friend, I come up to you and shake your hand warmly, would that give me assurance? Not really. But suppose you come up to me and initiate the handshake. Well, then I begin to have some assurance. And that is exactly the way it is with the sacrament of baptism. It was instituted by Christ. It is his sacramental sign to us. By it he expresses to us what he has done for us.

It is right here, incidentally, that we see something very important about the sacrament of baptism. Our Baptist friends feel that there is something very much lacking in infant baptism because it is received in a passive manner. When we were baptized as infants, we were not even aware of what was transpiring. However, far from detracting from the significance of the sacrament, this passivity really underlines it. The sacrament is not saying something about what I have done, but rather about what Christ has done for me. It is not something that *I* initiated, but something that *he* initiated. And it is precisely because it comes from his side that it is a valid sign of redemption. After all, our salvation comes from his side, alone. Long before I existed, Christ bore my sins on the cross. While I was still dead in trespasses and sins, I was quickened by the Holy Spirit. To have a sign that is simply given to me—and received in a passive manner—makes it all the more fitting as a sign of God's way of redemption.

When we see baptism, we are looking at outward washing. But it is not this outward washing that saves us (just as it is not a warm handshake that produces friendship). No, the outward washing is only a picture (we could say) of an inner and invisible washing. This inner, invisible washing has two parts. One part is objective. That is, it is based on something entirely outside of us. The guilt of our sin, which once stood there in the sight of God, has been removed by the merits of Christ's atonement. The other part does take place within us. Our sinful hearts—the source of our many sins—are renewed by the Holy Spirit.

Because of this, we begin once again to love God and keep his commandments. So, there is an objective side and a subjective side. There is the problem of my *guilt* (objective) and the problem of my innate *depravity* (subjective). And both of these are provided for in the saving work of the Lord Jesus. He took care of the one (the objective) when he paid off the debt for all my transgressions. He took care of the other (the subjective) when he sent his Holy Spirit to regenerate me in order that I might be able to come to faith and repentance.

It is clear from all this that the sign—by itself—has no power at all to save us. Some churches have taught that baptism saves because it is a divine act of cleansing. But we know that this is not biblical teaching. Under the Old Testament, circumcision was the sign and seal (Rom. 4:11) of the covenant, which has now been replaced by baptism (Col. 2:11). Yet we know that Abraham was converted *before* he received circumcision. But if Abraham was converted before he received the sign and seal, it is evident that the sign and seal could not have been the cause. We also know that there are people, such as Judas Iscariot, who have received the sign and seal, and who have yet remained unconverted. It just is not true that everyone who is baptized becomes a genuine Christian. It may be asked, then, why baptism is called *"the washing of regeneration"* in Titus 3:5. The answer is that there is a close relationship between the *outward* sign and the *inward* reality (of which it gives a representation) in Scripture.

Here, again, an illustration may help us understand this basic connection. Let us say that on a very hot day you pass a sign with a picture of a bottle of Coca-Cola. You turn to your friend and say, "Doesn't that Coke make you thirsty?" What you really mean, of course, is that the picture makes you think of a refreshing drink. You both understand this, in spite of the fact that you spoke as if you could drink what you saw in the picture. Well, that is also Paul's meaning when he says what he does about the water of baptism. He does not mean that baptism in and of itself can wash us with regeneration. He means that it is a picture of regeneration, and that we need what is set forth by the picture. But we will have more to say about this later.

Questions on the Lesson

1. Why is it important to stress that the sacraments are divinely instituted?

2. What is the primary error in the Baptist view of baptism?
3. What are the two essential parts of inward washing?
4. Prove that baptism, itself, does not save.

QUESTIONS FOR STUDY AND DISCUSSION

1. Is a person's heart renewed by the Holy Spirit at the same time as he is baptized? What biblical evidence can you give for your answer?
2. Since an infant is not aware of what is happening in his baptism, what good is it to him?
3. Is the promise that God gives in baptism even given to those who receive it without being true believers (e.g., Simon the sorcerer in Acts 8:9–25)?

LORD'S DAY 27

SCRIPTURE READINGS: *Genesis 17; Acts 2:39; Galatians 3:23–29; Colossians 2:11–12*

72. **Q.** **Is, then, the outward washing with water itself the washing away of sin?**

A. No, for only the blood of Jesus Christ and the Holy Spirit cleanse us from all sins.

73. **Q.** **Why, then, does the Holy Spirit call baptism *the washing of regeneration* and *the washing away of sins*?**

A. God speaks thus not without great cause: to wit, not only to teach us thereby that as the filthiness of the body is taken away by water, so our sins are removed by the blood and Spirit of Jesus Christ; but especially to assure us by this divine pledge and sign that we are spiritually cleansed from our sins as really as we are outwardly washed with water.

74. **Q.** **Are infants also to be baptized?**

A. Yes; for since they, as well as adults, are included in the covenant and Church of God, and since both redemption from sin and the Holy Spirit, the Author of faith, are through the blood of Christ promised to them no less than to adults, they must also by baptism, as a sign of the covenant, be ingrafted into the Christian Church, and distinguished from the children of unbelievers, as was done in the old covenant or testament by circumcision, instead of which baptism was instituted in the new covenant.

We have already anticipated some of the teaching of this section of the Catechism in previous lessons. For this reason we will simply try to give a little added emphasis to some of these truths here. The first important teaching is that there is no saving power in the sacrament itself. Now we might imagine that there is no need to emphasize this fact. After all, we are not Roman Catholics. So we do not believe in baptismal regeneration, do we? No, of course not. Yet the danger is not something imaginary, even for us. Let me illustrate what I mean. I once met a man who proudly stated that he had been baptized by the famous Abraham Kuyper (this happened many years ago, and the man was already up in years). Was there not in these remarks at least the hint of the idea that perhaps there was some special power in baptism? What we always need to keep clearly in mind is the fact that baptism is a God-ordained picture of the washing away of the sins of believers. It displays to us in a visible way our entrance into the saving grace of God in the Lord Jesus.

Why, then, does the apostle say that we are saved "*through the washing of regeneration and renewing of the Holy Spirit*" (Titus 3:5)? This is the second great truth expounded in this part of the Catechism. Baptism is called the washing of regeneration because there is a God-ordained relationship between the saving reality represented and the symbol that represents that reality. In other words, we should not think of baptism only in terms of the outward symbols. It is a God-ordained picture of the saving work of the Spirit of God.

We have already remarked that there is an ever-present danger of forgetting to make the needed distinction between the sign (baptism) and the thing signified (the saving work of God). But there is also the danger of trying to separate what God has joined together. For example, it is quite common today for Christian people to associate their conversion with something that has no basis in Scripture (such as an altar call at a revival meeting), rather than with baptism (with which it is always associated in Scripture). Today we would expect to hear someone say, "When I went forward that day, I clothed myself with Christ." But Paul does not say that. What he says is this: "*As many of you as were baptized into Christ have put on Christ*" (Gal. 3:27). And, "*As many of us as were baptized into Christ Jesus were baptized into His death*" (Rom. 6:3).

Take, for instance, a man who lives in a country dominated by Islam. If he dares to receive Christian baptism, he may well put his own life, and the lives of his children who are baptized with him, in danger.

Yet he knows that Christ says we must confess him before men if we are really going to be his disciples. Suppose, then, that this man determines that he would rather risk death than not have Jesus. So he and his children receive baptism. Can you imagine that *he* would ever separate the reality from the symbol? If you ask him, "When were you washed from your sins?" he would undoubtedly say, "It was when I and my covenant children received holy baptism." Yes, and he would be right, because baptism is the means chosen by God to assure us "that we are spiritually cleansed from our sins as really as we are outwardly washed with water." So, while we must distinguish between the sign and that which is signified, we must also remember never to separate them completely.

But why are infants baptized (if their parents are God's covenant people)? The answer in four simple words is: because God commanded it. This is the third great truth expounded in this part of the Catechism. The command is found in the book of Genesis (chap. 17). God commanded Abraham to give the covenant sign (which, at that time, was circumcision) both to himself and to his male children. He also said that this command would continue throughout all generations. When Jesus Christ came, as the true Messiah of God, he did not abrogate this covenant that God had made with Abraham. To the contrary, he confirmed it (see Gal. 3:15). But he did open that covenant up to men of all nations who receive him as the Messiah. That is why Scripture says, *"If you are Christ's, then you are Abraham's seed, and heirs according to the promise"* (Gal. 3:29). The only difference is that circumcision has now been replaced by water baptism (Col. 2:11–12) and is now applied to both males and females (Acts 8:12).

It is simply not true, then, as opponents of infant baptism claim, that there is no difference between the children of believers and the children of unbelievers. There *is* a difference. True, the Bible itself says that there is no difference *by nature*. But there is a difference *by grace*. Grace is God's unmerited favor. And God has graciously chosen to be a God to us and to our children (Acts 2:39). That is why there is a difference between our children and other children. The difference is that our children are brought up within the Lord's congregation. From the very first beginning of life they are "in the way" of the saving ordinances of God. They are under the Word and the sacraments. In a true church of Christ they will come to know the way of salvation. And that is not true, by far, of the children of unbelievers.

This does not mean that we may assume that our children are elect and regenerate. Neither, by the way, may we assume the opposite. God does not tell us to live on the basis of assumptions, but in the way of covenant faithfulness and hope in his promise. God certainly will preserve his church through the line of the generations. *"For the promise is to you and to your children,"* declared Peter, at the very threshold of the present era, *"as many as the Lord our God will call"* (Acts 2:39). Take a good look at the church today and you will see one thing quite clearly, if you are discerning. Most of those who constitute a faithful church today were nurtured within it as covenant children. Yes, by all means the sign of baptism must be given to children. This would not be the right thing to do, obviously, if salvation were not a gift from God, from start to finish. But that is exactly what it is. For *this* reason infant baptism now, like infant circumcision in Abraham's era, is an eloquent sign of what God does in saving his children.

QUESTIONS ON THE LESSON

1. Do Protestants sometimes believe the sacraments have saving power?
2. If baptism does not save, what is meant by Titus 3:5?
3. Why is it harmful to separate the sign from the thing signified?
4. Why do we baptize the children of believers?
5. Do we presume that covenant children are regenerate (or unregenerate)?

QUESTIONS FOR STUDY AND DISCUSSION

1. What harm comes from failing to distinguish baptism from what it signifies?
2. What will happen to our children if they die before they are baptized? Compare this to the Roman Catholic doctrine concerning infants who die before baptism.
3. If a child is not regenerate, what right do we have to baptism him and to call him a child of God?
4. Should we tell our children that they belong to God? Won't that produce in them false confidence of their salvation?

LORD'S DAY 28

SCRIPTURE READINGS: *Mark 14:22–24;*
1 Corinthians 10:16–17; 11:23–25; Hebrews 10:10–12

75. **Q. How is it signified and sealed unto you in the holy supper that you partake of the one sacrifice of Christ, accomplished on the cross, and of all His benefits?**

A. Thus, that Christ has commanded me and all believers to
eat of this broken bread and to drink of this cup in remembrance of Him, and has added these promises: first,
that His body was offered and broken on the cross for me,
and His blood shed for me, as certainly as I see with my
eyes the bread of the Lord broken for me, and the cup
communicated to me; and further, that with His crucified
body and shed blood He Himself feeds and nourishes my
soul to everlasting life as assuredly as I receive from the
hand of the minister, and taste with my mouth, the bread
and cup of the Lord as sure signs of the body and blood
of Christ.

76. **Q. What is it to eat the crucified body and drink the shed
blood of Christ?**

A. It is not only to embrace with a believing heart all the sufferings and the death of Christ, and thereby to obtain the
forgiveness of sins and life eternal, but, further, also to become more and more united to His sacred body, by the
Holy Spirit, who dwells both in Christ and in us, so that,
though Christ is in heaven and we are on earth, we are
nevertheless flesh of His flesh and bone of His bones, and

live and are governed by one Spirit, as members of the same body are by one soul.

77.   Q. Where has Christ promised that He will as certainly feed and nourish believers with His body and blood as they eat of this broken bread and drink of this cup?

A. In the institution of the supper, which reads thus: *The Lord Jesus in the night in which he was betrayed took bread; and when he had given thanks, he brake it, and said, This is my body, which is for you; this do in remembrance of me. In like manner also the cup, after supper, saying, This cup is the new covenant in my blood; this do, as often as ye drink it, in remembrance of me. For as often as ye eat this bread, and drink the cup, ye proclaim the Lord's death till he come,* 1 Cor. 11:23–26. This promise is repeated by St. Paul, where he says: *The cup of blessing which we bless, is it not a communion of the blood of Christ? The bread which we break, is it not a communion of the body of Christ? seeing that we, who are many, are one bread, one body; for we all partake of the one bread,* 1 Cor. 10:16, 17.

The Heidelberg Catechism is more detailed in its treatment of the Lord's Supper than it is with respect to any other doctrine. For this there is a very good reason. The Catechism was written at the time of the Reformation, when there was a strong consciousness of the errors of the Roman Catholic Church, from which the Reformers had been liberated. The Roman Catholic errors were then—and still are today—a very serious matter. And nowhere is this clearer or more important than right here in the doctrine of the Lord's Supper.

It was—and is—the teaching of the Roman Church that when the priest repeats the words *This is my body,* the bread is actually changed into the body of Christ. And again, when the priest takes the cup, it is the teaching of the Roman Church that the wine becomes the actual blood of Christ. But that is not all. Rome also says that in this act of transubstantiation (i.e., the changing of one substance into another) there is a real continuation of the sacrifice of Christ. But this teaching is certainly not true. In actual fact there is no change in the substance of the bread or the wine. The bread remains bread and the wine remains wine. There is no repetition or continuation at all of the one sacrifice of the Lord Jesus. No, the Bible is perfectly clear about that: *"We have been sanctified through the offering of the body of Jesus Christ once for all"* (Heb. 10:10); and, *"This Man, after He had offered one sacrifice for sins forever, sat down at the right hand of God"* (v.12).

"Well, then," someone may ask, "does this mean that Roman Catholics believe in the *real* presence of Christ in the sacrament and we do not?" The answer is no! We most certainly do believe in the presence of Christ in the sacrament, but it is a spiritual presence. That is to say, it is a presence mediated through the Holy Spirit. And it is the manner in which this takes place that is set forth in Answer 75.

There is no salvation—no spiritual life—for anyone except in connection with the body of Jesus offered on the cross and his blood poured out for the sins of his people. It is the purpose of the sacrament to help us "see" this. As we take the bread (and remember that it is bread) to nourish our bodies, we are also to believe in Jesus Christ and the work he has done as the sole ground of our salvation. And as we drink the wine (and it really is wine), we are to put our whole trust in the sacrifice of our Lord Jesus. There is, in other words, the visible (the sign and seal) and the invisible (the participation by faith in the redemptive benefits of Christ's one sacrifice). And, again, it is wrong either to *separate* the one from the other or to *confuse* the one with the other.

This fact is perfectly clear in the answer to Question 76, "What is it to eat . . . and drink?" It means to have union with Christ by faith and thus to share in the benefits of his one offering. Just as my hand takes the bread and the wine, and I eat it and am nourished by it, so my faith (you could call faith the hand of the soul) receives and rests on Jesus alone as my complete salvation. This is the real presence of Jesus. His presence is real because the same Holy Spirit of God that dwells in Christ (without measure) also dwells in me, so that I am united, the one with the other. There really is a common life—and a communal life—that I share with the Savior. But no one has this merely because of eating the bread or drinking the wine. That is why it is possible (as the apostle says in 1 Cor. 11:29) to eat and drink our own judgment! This is possible because one can have the sign and seal without the greater reality of which it is a picture.

Yet, the emphasis of Answer 77 is the proper one. The sacrament was not given to us so that we would have the external sign and seal while the "real thing" remains far away from us. No, the sacrament is a means of grace—it proclaims God's grace to sinners. The words of institution, quoted here, were not spoken to spiritual supermen. They were spoken to men with weaknesses like our own. They were spoken to assure them that wherever and whenever this sacrament is faithfully administered, there is a participation in the saving blessings of which it is a symbol. Let a man be one of the weakest in faith who ever lived— still, one thing is certain. He will participate in Christ's body and blood, if he believes, because that is the promise of Jesus to every believer. (Of course, Jesus promised nothing at all to an unbeliever such as Judas.)

The doctrine of transubstantiation is wrong. It is wrong because it confuses the created thing (bread and wine) with the Creator (Jesus). It is wrong because it makes it virtually unimportant whether or not one has faith in the Lord Jesus and his one sacrifice on the cross. It is also wrong because it demands faith in a so-called miracle (transubstantiation), which in fact never happens. It is little wonder that our reforming fathers spelled out the doctrine of the Lord's Supper in considerable detail.

QUESTIONS ON THE LESSON

1. Why is this part of the Catechism more detailed than other parts?
2. Show from Scripture that there can be no repetition or continuation of the sacrifice of Christ.
3. Do Reformed Christians believe in a real presence of Christ in the Lord's Supper? Explain.
4. Of what may even the weakest believer be certain?

QUESTIONS FOR STUDY AND DISCUSSION

1. What is the significance of *eating* the bread and *drinking* the wine in the Lord's Supper? Why not just look at these symbols?
2. Why do you think the idea arose that the sacrament of the Lord's Supper is a continuation or repetition of Christ's sacrifice on the cross?
3. Why is the doctrine of transubstantiation and the so-called real presence of Christ so important to the Roman Catholic Church?

LORD'S DAY 29

SCRIPTURE READINGS: *1 Corinthians 10:3-4; John 6:26–59*

78. **Q.** Do, then, the bread and wine become the real body and blood of Christ?

A. No; but as the water in baptism neither is changed into the blood of Christ, nor is the washing away of sins itself, being only the divine token and confirmation thereof, so likewise the bread in the Lord's supper does not become the real body of Christ, though agreeably to the nature and property of sacraments it is called the body of Christ Jesus.

79. **Q.** Why, then, does Christ call the bread *His body,* and the cup *His blood* or *the new covenant in His blood,* and Paul, *a communion of the body and blood of Christ?*

A. Christ speaks thus not without great cause; namely, not only to teach us thereby that, as bread and wine sustain this temporal life, so also His crucified body and shed blood are the true food and drink of our souls unto eternal life; but much more, by these visible signs and pledges to assure us that we are as really partakers of His true body and blood, through the working of the Holy Spirit, as we receive by the mouth of the body these holy tokens in remembrance of Him; and that all His sufferings and obedience are as certainly ours as if we ourselves had in our own persons suffered and made satisfaction to God for our sins.

Is there really any need to argue for the truth of Q/A 78? On the night in which our Lord was betrayed, says the gospel account, he took bread and distributed it, saying, *"This is My body"* (Matt. 26:26). Does anyone think that something happened, at that instant, to the body of Jesus? Did the body of Jesus disappear so that it could take the form of bread? Did the blood of Christ leave the veins of his body? Was part of his blood in the body of Christ and another part in the cup he passed to his disciples? To ask such questions is to answer them, because they need no answer. It is self-evident that when Jesus spoke these words, he meant that the bread and wine *represented* his body and blood.

At one time I lived a few miles from a large city. When I drove into that city by the usual route, a certain sign was always visible. It showed a man drinking a glass of fresh fruit juice. It was a very realistic picture. As a matter of fact, whenever that sign came into view, I felt a sensation of thirst. As I looked at that picture, I could almost taste the fresh juice. Of course, that was the purpose of the sign. It was put there to make people thirsty enough to go right out and buy some of the advertised product.

It is much the same with the sacraments. Water, in the sacrament of baptism, does not itself wash away sin. But it does present a vivid picture. Again, the bread and the wine used in the sacrament of the Lord's Supper are not themselves the sacrifice of Jesus. But they do present a vivid picture, reminding us of it. As a matter of fact, the picture is so vivid that we ought to think of the one as soon as we see the other. We ought to think of what our Lord did on the cross at the moment we see the bread and the wine given. At the same time, we should not ignore the difference between the sign and the thing that is pictured.

The Catechism speaks of the "nature and property of sacraments." This means that the association between the sign and the thing signified is so close that we can call the one by the name of the other. Let us again try to illustrate. Two men are walking along on a hot day in the city. They are getting more and more thirsty. One of them looks up and sees a big picture of a cold drink and says, "Man, I wish I had that." Now, of course he doesn't mean that literally. What he wants is not a picture of a drink. What he really means is that he wishes he had the drink pictured on the billboard.

This is what the Catechism means when it speaks of "the nature and property of sacraments." It means that we commonly speak of the one, using the name of the other. Jesus, for example, said *"I am the bread of life"* (John 6:35). Now, literally speaking, Jesus is not a loaf of bread. But we know what he meant. Again, on the night of the Last Supper, he took bread and said, *"This is My body."* He did not mean that the bread was no longer bread or that it had become his own body. He simply meant that the bread that he held in his hand *represented* his body.

As Q/A 79 shows, there is good reason why the Lord Jesus spoke in this manner. He did it to strengthen or reinforce the closeness of the association. Suppose, for a moment, that Jesus had said, "This is my bread, broken for you." Do you not see how much weaker it would have been? It would have been like a sign that said "Here, have a picture of a Coke," instead of "Here, have a Coke." What a difference. Christ spoke as he did so that we would always associate the one with the other and realize that we must never, ever, try to separate them from each other. Christ intended the visible sign and seal to go with the invisible reality of union with Jesus. When I see a picture of a Coke, it does not make me want a picture—I want "the real thing" itself. And when I see the picture of Christ's body and blood, I don't want just the bread and the wine, but "the real thing" that it represents. And that is salvation through Christ's great atonement.

Like all illustrations, the one that we have used here is not perfect. It fails at one important point. When you see the picture of a Coke, it makes you want one, but you can't always find a place that has one (no, not always). But this is not true when it comes to "the real thing" in the sacrament of the Lord's Supper. All you need is a genuine hunger and thirst after righteousness, because Jesus said that all who have such will be satisfied (Matt. 5:6). Christ is the bread and the water of life, and all who hunger and thirst for him will have eternal salvation (and that *is* the real thing).

Where the gospel is preached and the sacraments are rightly administered, there Christ himself is presented. And to hunger and thirst after him is really one and the same with real eating and drinking. Let us put it this way: when you see that sign with a picture of a Coke, you get thirsty—but that doesn't mean that you actually have your drink. With the sacrament it is different. When you take the bread and the wine, hungering and thirsting for union with the Lord Jesus Christ, you have it. You have it because that hunger and thirst is itself a reaching out to the Lord Jesus—and no one ever does that without receiving eternal salvation.

There is, then, a sacramental relationship between the one (the bread/wine) and the other (the body/blood). It is a relationship appointed by Christ himself, and we must not separate what he has joined together. It is this point that is so powerfully stated in Q/A 79. The way in which bread and wine nourish our temporal life is an image of the way in which we are nourished with eternal life by Christ's sacrifice offered to the Father. The one represents the other. Not only that, but he assures us of the one (the nourishment of eternal life) by means of the other (the nourishment of the physical body). It will perhaps help if we illustrate what would happen if we separated the one from the other.

A man is driving along in his car. He sees a sign along the highway. It warns him of a railroad crossing ahead. It does this by using an X to picture a crossing. It is there to represent something further down the road, beyond his range of vision. As long as there really is a railroad crossing ahead, the sign has a valuable function. But I once knew of some high school students who moved such a sign from where it originally was to another location. That was a very serious thing, because the people who approached the railroad crossing had no warning, and the people who saw the sign (out of place) were needlessly alerted.

The same thing is possible when it comes to the Lord's Supper. If a person takes the Lord's Supper without remembering and believing in the Lord's sacrifice, he only receives the sign, and that results in his own judgment. But if a person does remember and believe in the Lord's sacrifice, he receives both the sign of the sacrament and the spiritual reality. This is what the sign was intended to do for us. God wants us to partake of the spiritual reality just as certainly as we do of the physical elements. The visible sign was given in order to assure us of the invisible reality.

QUESTIONS ON THE LESSON

1. What did not happen when Christ instituted the Lord's Supper?
2. What do we need to understand about sacramental language?
3. Is there any analogy to this in everyday life?
4. In one vital point all illustrations fail. What is that point in the Coke illustration?
5. Why is it important to avoid identifying the sign with the thing signified?
6. Why is it important to avoid separating the sign from the thing signified?

Questions for Study and Discussion

1. Think of some other situations in which we use symbolic language (i.e., using a term to refer to that which it symbolizes).
2. Since the idea that bread and wine are actually changed into the body and blood of Christ is so contrary to reason and common sense, how did this teaching arise?
3. Why does Jesus use such striking, even coarse, language in John 6:53–58?

LORD'S DAY 30

80. **Q. What difference is there between the Lord's supper and the popish mass?**

A. The Lord's supper testifies to us that we have full pardon of all our sins by the only sacrifice of Jesus Christ, which He Himself has once accomplished on the cross; and that by the Holy Spirit we are ingrafted into Christ, who according to His human nature is now not on earth but in heaven, at the right hand of God His Father, and wills there to be worshipped by us; but the mass teaches that the living and the dead have not the forgiveness of sins through the sufferings of Christ unless Christ is still daily offered for them by the priests; and that Christ is bodily present under the form of bread and wine and is therefore to be worshipped in them. And thus the mass, at bottom, is nothing else than a denial of the one sacrifice and passion of Jesus Christ, and an accursed idolatry.

Here is one of the places in which the Heidelberg Catechism has been criticized. It has been criticized because the final part of the answer calls the Roman Catholic Mass "an accursed idolatry." It has been criticized for two reasons. First, this was not part of the original text of the Catechism but was added later. Second, some people feel that language like this gives needless offense. "Is it really necessary," they ask, "to use the term *idolatry* when speaking of Roman Catholic worship?"

In answer to this, we would point out that there is nothing more central to true Christian teaching than the doctrine of the atonement.

Jesus died. He died for sinners. He died only once. He died in order to pay the complete price for all the sins of his people. *"Now, once at the end of the ages, He has appeared to put away sin by the sacrifice of Himself"* (Heb. 9:26). Yes, *"Christ was offered once to bear the sins of many"* (v. 28), for *"by one offering He has perfected forever those who are being sanctified"* (10:14) (emphasis added).

Since the Mass claims to be a sacrifice—a continuation of the sacrifice of Jesus—it detracts from the honor and glory of Christ's finished work. But that is not all. It is also the teaching of the Mass that the bread and wine are transformed into the body and blood of Jesus. The sacramental elements are said to become the actual body and blood of Christ, making it perfectly proper to adore and worship them. And that *is* idolatry, because it gives to a created thing the worship that belongs to the Creator alone.

The doctrine of transubstantiation is not true. The wine and bread are not changed into the blood and body of Jesus. So, when the priest makes this false claim and holds up the cup as if it were divine, it is idolatrous worship. Idolatry is the worship of something other than the only true God, as if it were divine. If we worship a statue of wood or stone as if it were divine, that is idolatrous worship. This is exactly what happens in Roman Catholic worship. Therefore, it was altogether proper to add the last sentence to Answer 80. It is true, of course, that one could infer this last statement from the facts already stated in the first part of this answer. When we understand what the Lord's Supper really is—and compare this with Roman Catholic teaching—we realize that it is basically a denial of Christ's perfect atonement and a type of idolatrous worship. But since people don't always think through implications and draw the appropriate conclusions, it was wise to spell this out so that no one could miss it.

One could put it like this: the purpose of the Lord's Supper is to *prevent* the blasphemy of idolatrous worship. When we eat and drink in remembrance of him and what he did once for all for his people, we realize that there is no room anymore for a sacrificing priesthood. The fact that the Roman Catholic Church has a priestly order advertises its idolatrous nature. It says by that very fact that the one sacrifice of Christ on the cross wasn't sufficient. But it *was* sufficient. That's why Jesus said that we were to *"proclaim* [or show forth]" his death until he comes (1 Cor. 11:26). We show it forth when we realize that it is perfect and completely sufficient. What we have, in other words, is union with

Christ himself, who is now at the right hand of the Father. We partic-ipate in the benefits of that one perfect oblation which he offered to his Father.

Under the Old Testament, a special priestly order was appropriate because daily sacrifices were needed. They were needed because God's people sinned every day in thought, word, and deed. Animal sacrifices had to be repeated again and again, because they had only a limited value. They pointed forward, however, to that wonderful day when there would be one final and all-sufficient atonement. For the Roman Catholic Church to have a priestly class now, claiming that continuing sacrifice is still needed, is really to deny what Jesus has done and to put the crea-ture in the place of the Creator. So the problem isn't in the Catechism, but rather in the people who don't like to face up to the truth and call things by their true name. It may offend. It may be unpleasant to hear. But the Catechism has one big advantage. It is true. The Mass is a de-nial of the one sacrifice of Jesus and an accursed idolatry.

QUESTIONS ON THE LESSON

1. Does Answer 80 go too far in what it says about Roman Catholic worship?
2. What does the doctrine of transubstantiation teach?
3. What biblical data prove that this is a false teaching?

QUESTIONS FOR STUDY AND DISCUSSION

1. During the Reformation, did the Roman Church consider the doc-trine of the Mass to be a doctrine essential to salvation? Does it still?
2. Should we tell Roman Catholics that their church teaches and prac-tices "an accursed idolatry"?
3. What connection is there between the doctrine of the Mass and the doctrine of a continuing priesthood?
4. Does the doctrine of the Mass have anything to do with the lack of godliness in the lives of so many Roman Catholics?

LORD'S DAY 30—CONTINUED

SCRIPTURE READINGS: *1 Corinthians 10:19–22; 11:17–34*

81. Q. For whom is the Lord's supper instituted?

A. For those who are truly displeased with themselves for their sins and yet trust that these are forgiven them for the sake of Christ, and that their remaining infirmity is covered by His passion and death; who also desire more and more to strengthen their faith and amend their life. But hypocrites and such as turn not to God with sincere hearts eat and drink judgment to themselves.

82. Q. Are they also to be admitted to this supper who, by their confession and life, show themselves to be unbelieving and ungodly?

A. No; for in this way the covenant of God would be profaned and His wrath kindled against the whole congregation; wherefore the Christian Church is in duty bound, according to the ordinance of Christ and His apostles, to exclude such persons by the keys of the kingdom of heaven, until they show amendment of life.

This section of the Heidelberg Catechism is certainly at variance with the view that now prevails in most Protestant churches, even those that are more conservative. The practice of "open communion" is widely accepted. When the Lord's Supper is administered in most Protestant churches today, only a verbal warning is given that only true believers ought to come to the table. It is then left entirely to each individual to judge whether or not he or she *is* a genuine believer and therefore may rightfully participate. What a shock it is, then, for those who attend a communion service in a church that is faithful to the teaching of the Catechism. In such a church, it is not left to the individual alone to decide this question. No, in such a church the elders allow no one to come who is not certified beforehand to be a baptized Christian living a consistent Christian life. This is commonly called "restricted communion."

As Answer 81 makes clear, this does not mean that the importance of individual self-examination is in any way diminished. Not at all. And it is still the responsibility of the minister to warn all who profess faith in Christ to examine themselves (1 Cor. 11:28; 2 Cor. 13:5). The reason for this is that there are hypocrites, that is, people who profess to belong to Christ but who actually have no union with him. This is tragic, but it is true. And it is the will of the Lord that this fact be known, and that we reckon with it. On the night in which he was betrayed, our Lord already knew who would betray him. John says that Jesus knew this right from the beginning (John 6:64). But all he said to the disciples that night was that one of them would betray him. He could have told them, of course, who that one was. And had he done so, none of the others would have had any reason for deep concern. However, when Jesus simply told them that one of them would do it, each began at once to consider his own spiritual condition. "*Lord, is it I?*" they each began to ask (Matt. 26:22). And that was exactly the effect intended by Jesus. He wanted them to examine themselves. And when we observe the Lord's Supper today, the minister ought to have the same purpose. We should make it clear that no one is really welcome to come to the Lord's Table except those who are repentant ("displeased with themselves for their sins") and truly believing (trusting "that [their sins] are forgiven them for the sake of Christ"). There ought to be a very clear warning that hypocrites, by playing a pious role but having no real faith in Christ, incur God's judgment.

Yet, as the Catechism shows us in Q/A 82, this is *not* all there is to it. No, there is also a responsibility that rests on the church as a covenant community. And that responsibility is to exercise the keys of the kingdom—one aspect of which is to exclude from the Lord's Table those who, by the way they talk and live, show that they have no part in God's kingdom. Or, to say the same thing positively, the church has the responsibility of admitting to the Lord's Table those who show by the way they talk and live that they *are* godly people. Now it is an odd fact that this authority is rather generally recognized when it comes to the sacrament of baptism. It has been our experience, at least, that very few people seem to think that just anyone who pleases can come forward in the church service and be baptized on his own responsibility alone. People expect the church to have at least some requirements that must be met first by those who request baptism. Yet, for some reason, the same people expect the church to administer the other sacrament (the Lord's Supper) to people without insisting on any requirements by which the church judges their right to participate.

Sometimes people will be offended (in the sense that they will not like it) if the church insists on restricting admission to the Lord's Table. But the church must stand firm in this, not only for the sake of its own faithfulness to Christ—and the meaning of the Lord's Supper—but also for the sake of the very ones who are (for the time being) excluded.

In the early years of my ministry, I relied entirely on verbal instruction and individual self-examination to keep away from the Lord's Table those who would harm themselves by partaking. At that time there was a young man who visited the church, and after hearing the words of warning, he partook of the Lord's Supper. Later on it became quite clear (even to him) that his understanding of the gospel was very limited. He simply did not grasp the meaning of the words of warning. As he himself later said, "It all sounded good to me, at the time, so I thought I should partake." Yet, as he later came to see himself, he did not understand Christ's sacrifice. He had not repented and did not yet believe, and so he should not have come to the table. But who was at fault that this young man ate and drank in an unworthy manner? Was it *his* fault? Or was it really the fault of the pastor and elders, who knew what a serious thing this was and how wrong it was for someone to come to the Lord's Table in ignorance? The answer is clear, and we did not try to evade it. We faced up to our responsibility and changed our way of administering the Lord's Supper. From that time on we only admitted to the Lord's Supper those who showed—by what they said, and by the way they lived—that they were genuine Christians.

Now of course this will never guarantee that all hypocrites will be excluded from the Lord's Supper. There was (as we have already pointed out) at least one hypocrite (Judas) in the purest church that ever existed, under the only perfect pastor in history, the Lord Jesus. Yet no one was admitted by our Lord to that supper who did not make a credible profession. (Judas knew the truth and professed allegiance to Jesus, just like the others.) Again, no one was admitted to the first celebration of this sacrament who did not appear to live as a Christian. (Even Judas did—in fact he made a great show of concern for the poor.) The Catechism is right in its teaching. It is vital both that the individual examine himself and that the church insist upon a credible profession prior to admittance to the Lord's Table. The neglect or denial of either of these will open the way to degeneration, while a faithful stress on both will bring us great blessing.

QUESTIONS ON THE LESSON

1. What is open communion?
2. What is restricted communion?
3. With which of these is the prevailing practice of baptism in harmony?
4. Does the practice of restricted communion diminish the importance of self-examination?
5. What harm is there in the practice of open communion?
6. Will the practice of restricted communion prevent all hypocrites from coming to the Lord's Table?

QUESTIONS FOR STUDY AND DISCUSSION

1. Discuss the prevalent view that the church consists of everyone who believes in Christ, regardless of whether they are members of a faithful church or not. Do you think that this view lies behind the common practice of open communion?
2. What standard should be used to determine whether visitors to the church should be allowed to come to the Lord's Table?
3. Do you think it is proper for people who disagree on some important doctrines to commune together at the Lord's Table? Can they commune as though they are one when their respective churches are divided on these doctrines?

LORD'S DAY 31

SCRIPTURE READINGS: *Matthew 16:17–20; 18:15–20;*
Hebrews 13:17; Titus 1:5–9

83. **Q.** **What are the keys of the kingdom of heaven?**

A. The preaching of the holy gospel, and church discipline or excommunication out of the Christian Church. By these two the kingdom of heaven is opened to believers and shut against unbelievers.

84. **Q.** **How is the kingdom of heaven opened and shut by the preaching of the holy gospel?**

A. By proclaiming and openly witnessing, according to the command of Christ, to believers, one and all, that, whenever they receive the promise of the gospel by a true faith, all their sins are really forgiven them of God for the sake of Christ's merits; and on the contrary, by proclaiming and witnessing to all unbelievers and such as do not sincerely repent that the wrath of God and eternal condemnation abide on them so long as they are not converted. According to this witness of the gospel God will judge, both in this life and in that which is to come.

85. **Q.** **How is the kingdom of heaven shut and opened by church discipline?**

A. By forbidding, according to the command of Christ, the use of the sacraments by those who under the Christian name maintain unchristian doctrines or practices; who will not, after repeated brotherly admonitions, renounce their

> errors and wicked course of life; and who, having been complained of to the church, or to those who are thereunto appointed by the church, despise their admonitions—by which censure they are excluded from the Christian Church, and by God himself from the kingdom of Christ; and by again receiving such as members of Christ and His Church when they promise and show real amendment.

What did Jesus mean when he said that he would give *"the keys of the kingdom"?* to Peter (Matt. 16:19)—and to the other apostles (Matt. 18:18; John 20:23)? The answer is found in the book of Acts and in several New Testament epistles. When Christ was about to ascend to heaven, he told his disciples to wait until the Holy Spirit was given (Luke 24:49). This they did. When the great event took place, as recorded in Acts 2, the apostle Peter began to open and close the kingdom of heaven. He did this in two ways. First, there was faithful preaching. The mighty sermon of Peter on the Day of Pentecost ended when the people were so *"cut to the heart"* (Acts 2:37) that they cried out. They wanted to know what to do, and Peter told them. He told them to repent and be baptized, and he said that those who yielded submission to the Word would receive the gift of the Holy Spirit. What was this, if it was not to open the kingdom of heaven to men? It is clear, in other words, that one of the keys of the kingdom is faithful preaching.

Second, there is church discipline. We have a good example of this in 1 Corinthians 5. A member of the Corinthian church was living in sin. It was a sin so scandalous that even the ungodly world condemned it. Yet the church had let the matter go. This permissive attitude Paul rebuked (v. 2). Then he went on to instruct them. He told them that they were to meet together in the name of Christ and that he, in spirit, would be with them. Then they were to *"deliver such a one to Satan"* (v. 5). The purpose of this act of discipline was of course to restore the offender. They were to exclude this man from the church in order *"that his spirit [might] be saved in the day of the Lord Jesus"* (v. 5). They were, in other words, to act in the hope that even if the man's sinful flesh was destroyed, his spirit would yet be saved on the Day of Judgment. As it turned out (2 Cor. 2:5–8), the man repented and was restored. But the point we make here is that it was by means of church discipline that this was accomplished. So this is the other key of the kingdom.

No one can hear the Word of God faithfully preached without one of two results. Paul says, *"We are to God the fragrance of Christ among those who are being saved and among those who are perishing. To the one we are the aroma of death to death, and to the other the aroma of life to life"* (2 Cor. 2:15–16). When the truth of God is faithfully preached, there is more than a man speaking. God himself speaks through the man (1 Thess. 2:3), and what he says is never "null and void" but effectual. So, in authentic preaching, whenever there is a call to repentance and faith, one of two things will follow. Those who act in the obedience of faith are thereby admitted to the kingdom of God, and those who do not are excluded. This is not mere theory. It is a fact. God has said, *"My word . . . that goes forth from My mouth . . . shall not return to Me void, but it shall accomplish what I please, and it shall prosper in the thing for which I sent it"* (Isa. 55:11).

Church discipline is an awesome thing, even though it is despised in much of the visible church today. The attitude of many people today toward church discipline is something like this: "Who do these elders think they are, claiming the power to put people out of the kingdom? They may be able to put people out of *their* church, but they can't put people out of *God's* kingdom." Yes, this view is all too common. If church discipline could be voted on, it would probably be voted out in most American churches! But truth is not determined by majority vote. It is determined by the will of God and of Jesus. And what did Jesus say? He said to Peter, *"Whatever you shall bind on earth shall have been bound in heaven, and whatever you shall loose on earth shall have been loosed in heaven"* (Matt. 16:19, NASB). It is important to note that the verdict of heaven is not dependent on the verdict of Peter. No, it is the other way around. Peter's verdict, if it is to have effect, must be in agreement with the already determined verdict of heaven. But it is right here that we see the power! When Peter acted in a faithful way, his verdict was in agreement with heaven. And when ruling elders today are in agreement with heaven, their decisions are also effectual. When the church exercises discipline according to the Word of God, it is really a declaration of the mind of Christ. And it *is*, therefore, authoritative.

When a judge sentences a man to death, the power of the state, which is the power of the sword, stands behind his declaration. The judge has no power in and of himself. But he has great power when he faithfully executes the law of the land. So do church rulers who follow the Scriptures. All church power (as our fathers used to say) is ministerial and declarative. This means that the elders have no inherent power in themselves. The power is resident only in the person of Christ. An ambassador has no inherent power. The power belongs wholly to the government that he represents. But so long as he faithfully represents that government, no one can deny that there is power in what he says. So, let people laugh at church discipline if they choose. Let them say, "Who do they think they are to put people out of the church?" If these elders are acting in accord with the Bible, the power of heaven stands behind what they say and no amount of ridicule or scoffing can change this.

One of the greatest problems in the church today is its divisions. This situation has made it much easier for people to scoff at the power of the keys of the kingdom. If a faithful church makes use of the keys, those who are guilty can easily find another church that will accept them. And the painful fact is that the other church will often receive people who are fleeing from discipline as if they are poor victims, rather than culprits. There is an urgent need for all churches that are striving to be faithful to the Bible to take care that they do not undermine each other's discipline.

QUESTIONS ON THE LESSON

1. Jesus spoke of "the keys of the kingdom." How do we know what they are?
2. What differences are there between these two keys of the kingdom?
3. On what does the actual power of church discipline on earth depend?
4. Why has effective church discipline become so difficult today?

QUESTIONS FOR STUDY AND DISCUSSION

1. Since the gospel is the good news of salvation, how can we say that the preaching of the gospel closes the kingdom to some?
2. If we put people who are unfaithful under church discipline, won't that harden them all the more and drive them further from the church? Wouldn't it be better to let such people remain members in good standing in the hope that at least they will keep coming to hear the preaching of God's Word?
3. What results are seen in churches that neglect church discipline over many years?

PART III

GRATITUDE

LORD'S DAY 32

SCRIPTURE READINGS: *1 John 3:10–15; 5:1–5*

At this point in the Catechism we begin a new section. But before deal-
ing with the particulars, we look briefly at some of the general features.

One of the impressive things in the Heidelberg Catechism is the
fact that the Ten Commandments are dealt with in the third section.
(The Westminster Shorter Catechism also expounds the law *after* it
teaches the way of salvation.) This fact itself contains a volume of
teaching. You see, one might have expected that the Ten Commandments would be dealt with in Part I of the Catechism. In a general
way they are, of course, for Q/A 3 teaches that the law of God shows
me how great my sin and misery are. Why, then, does the Catechism
refer (in Q/A 4) only to the summary of the law? And why does it
wait until Q/A 92 in Part III before it treats the Ten Commandments
in detail?

The answer is that the men who wrote the Heidelberg Catechism
were aware of a great danger—the danger of thinking that we need the
law of God before we are justified to show us our need of the Savior,
but that we don't need it afterwards. Of course, one important use of
the law is to show us our need for salvation. However, we continue to
have this need after we are justified. Through the law of God we learn
all the days of our lives to understand more and more clearly that we
are unworthy sinners. And then, on top of that, there is yet another use
of the law. The law shows us, as the people of God, how we ought to
live in gratitude for our salvation. The Catechism, by expounding the
law at this point, underlines the importance of these three beneficial
uses of the law, and at the same time it warns against the dangerous error of lawlessness.

86.   **Q. Since, then, we are delivered from our misery by grace
alone, through Christ, without any merit of ours, why
must we yet do good works?**

   A. Because Christ, having redeemed us by His blood, also re-
   news us by His Holy Spirit after His own image, that with
   our whole life we may show ourselves thankful to God for
   His benefits, and that He may be praised by us; then, also,
   that each of us may be assured in himself of his faith by
   the fruits thereof, and that by our godly walk our neighbors also may be won for Christ.

87.   **Q. Can they, then, not be saved who, continuing in their
wicked and ungrateful lives, do not turn to God?**

   A. By no means; for the Scripture declares that no unchaste
   person, idolater, adulterer, thief, covetous man, drunkard,
   slanderer, robber, or any such like, shall inherit the kingdom of God.

There are those who say that Christians are under no obligation to keep
God's commandments. "No," they say, "we are saved by grace alone, and
therefore we are not under the law." It is perfectly true that we are justified only by free grace, and that our works do not enter in to our justification. But it is *not* true that this is all there is to say about God's plan
of salvation. To the contrary, the Bible says that salvation is something
stupendous. It not only changes how a man stands before God legally
(when he is justified), but also changes the man who has this standing.
He is regenerated by God and sanctified throughout his whole nature.

    Conceptually, these things can be separated, as if justification alone
were the whole of salvation. But in real people who are being saved,
these things cannot be separated from one another. A man who is saved
not only is justified through the atonement of Jesus, but also has the
law of God written in his heart through the work of the Holy Spirit
(Heb. 8:8–10). The men who wrote the Heidelberg Catechism understood this. To them it was simply unthinkable that one could really have
the one without the other. If you really are saved, their argument runs,
then radical changes will follow. They will follow because the Holy
Spirit of Christ is at work in the hearts of his people (Q/A 86).

    If all this is true, as the Catechism says, then why does it ask Ques-
tion 87: "Can they, then, not be saved who, continuing in their wicked

and ungrateful lives, do not turn to God?" This question is asked for the same reason that questions like this are asked in Scripture. People need to be warned that we cannot be saved without a radical change in our way of living. Notice how often the apostles themselves write about this very concern (1 Cor. 6:9–10; Gal. 5:13–26; Eph. 5:1–20; 1 John 3:4). The danger here is very real precisely because it is so appealing. It is natural for man to think that he can be justified by faith without any big changes in the way he lives. But the Bible is right, and the Catechism here simply echoes its warning. There is no salvation for those who remain unchanged, but only for those who in gratitude strive to keep God's commandments. The apostle John has truly said, *"This is the love of God, that we keep His commandments"* (1 John 5:3). That is why the law of God, as summarized in the Ten Commandments, is set forth for Christian believers as the great model for their life of gratitude.

Please take note of another thing here: the Heidelberg Catechism makes it clear that there are *ten* commandments. Sometimes today an attempt is made to eliminate the fourth commandment. The argument for this view runs something like this: Christ fulfilled this commandment for us, so we no longer have the duty to keep it. It is true, thank God, that the Lord Jesus *did* fulfill this commandment for us. But that is true of all the commandments—the one as much as the other. So the fact that the fourth commandment has been fulfilled does not imply that it has been removed. We will say more about this when we consider what the Catechism says about this commandment. Here we only want to point out that the Catechism sees the whole law (and all ten commandments as a summary of it) as an unbreakable unit.

Finally, note that the Catechism weaves some of the Old Testament "case law" materials into its exposition of the Ten Commandments. Today, those who do this are often taken to task for insisting that there is an abiding principle in every single case law in the books of Moses. We are thinking here of Reformed pastors and teachers who are often called theonomists. The word *theonomy* comes from two Greek words meaning "God" (*theos*) and "law" (*nomos*). I have no desire at all to be called a theonomist, because this word is used with too many conflicting definitions. But when it is used as a label for people who believe that the whole Bible—and every case law in the Bible—has authority and relevance for God's people, then I will accept the label, too. The point we want to make here is simply that the Heidelberg Catechism itself *is* "theonomic"—if by that we mean that Old Testament laws still have authority for God's people.

The amazing thing to me is that those who criticize this use of Old Testament case law have radically departed from the teaching of John Calvin. Calvin wrote one of the greatest commentaries that has ever been produced on the five books of Moses. And one of the things he does again and again in that work is to show how the case laws reveal principles that are still valid today for God's people. That doesn't mean that people today live in the same way they did in Moses' day, or that the case laws can be applied today without any changes. Of course, now there is a difference between riding a mule and flying in a jet airplane— a big difference. But the basic, underlying principles found in the Old Testament case laws are still valid. They still give us the analogies we need to understand God's will in our modern context. We will see that this was simply assumed by the authors of the Heidelberg Catechism.

QUESTIONS ON THE LESSON

1. Why does the Catechism treat the Ten Commandments in this final section, rather than after Q/A 3?
2. To what false presumption might the doctrine of justification by itself lead us if it is misunderstood?
3. Prove from Scripture that obedience to the law is in no way contrary to salvation by grace.
4. How many of the Ten Commandments does the Catechism regard as valid for us today?
5. What are the "case laws" of the Old Testament?
6. Are the case laws valid for us today?

QUESTIONS FOR STUDY AND DISCUSSION

1. Why is there a lack of emphasis on the Ten Commandments in non-Reformed churches?
2. Show that all ten of the commandments are restated or implied in New Testament texts.
3. Give some examples of how the principles in the commands given in Exodus 22:1–15 might be applied today.

LORD'S DAY 33

SCRIPTURE READINGS: *Ephesians 2:1–10; Mark 7:1–13*

88. **Q.** **Of how many parts does true conversion, or the turning of man to God, consist?**
   A. Two: the mortification of the old man, and the quickening of the new.

89. **Q.** **What is the mortification of the old man?**
   A. It is heartfelt sorrow that we have provoked God by our sins, and more and more to hate them and flee from them.

90. **Q.** **What is the quickening of the new man?**
   A. It is heartfelt joy in God through Christ, and with love and delight to live according to the will of God in all good works.

91. **Q.** **But what are good works?**
   A. Only those which are done from true faith, according to the law of God, and to His glory; and not such as are based on our own opinions or the precepts of men.

There is no salvation for the unconverted. That is why our Lord told Nicodemus that he had to be *"born again"* to see, and enter, the kingdom of God (John 3:1–8). If we are by nature dead in trespasses and sins (Eph. 2:1–3), then we are in need of radical change. This change is what takes place in us when we are converted. And the Catechism, using terms that are very close to those of the Bible itself, describes the two aspects of this great change.

On the one hand there is the dying away of the old self, and on the other hand there is the coming to life of the new. Each of these two aspects is viewed in two ways in the Bible: as already accomplished and as yet unfinished. Thus, both the dying away and the coming to life can be spoken of as already accomplished in the believer. In his letter to the Colossians, for example, Paul says, *"You have put off the old man with his deeds, and have put on the new man"* (3:9–10). Yet a few sentences earlier he says, *"Therefore put to death your members which are on the earth"* (3:5). From this it is quite clear that when a person is converted, something utterly decisive happens. It is so decisive, in fact, that such a person becomes *"a new creation"* (2 Cor. 5:17). Yet, at the same time, this radical change does not instantly produce what we might call a finished product of God's grace. No, the finished product comes only through a process of sanctification. And in that process of sanctification there is a continuation, a perfecting, of these two things.

How, then, can a person know that he is truly converted? The answer is found in his attitude toward sin and self, on the one hand, and toward God and Christ, on the other. When a person really is converted, there will be a complete reassessment of self. Before conversion, such a person would tend to defend himself against the accusations of conscience and the law of God. After conversion, a person accuses himself. After conversion, sin is no longer looked upon as a mere mistake. There is no longer an attempt to minimize sin by thinking (and often saying), "Well, we are all sinners." In a genuine conversion, a person comes to agree with God's point of view. When a sinner begins to see his sin as God sees it, there will be genuine sorrow and hatred of that sin. And there will be a radical turning away from it. At the same time, there will be a sense of wonder and amazement that God, even though he hates sin, loved us so much that he made a way of escape for us. So there will be an overflowing heart of gratitude, praise, and adoration of God for giving Christ to die for us, and of Christ for doing what he did to save us.

The proof of this conversion is found in one simple thing: "love and delight to live according to the will of God in all good works." How could it be otherwise? How could anyone really come to see himself as deserving hell, and the great sacrifice of Christ as the source of his complete pardon, without a deep sense of gratitude? How could anyone really have gratitude without being (as we learned in Q/A 1) "heartily willing and ready, henceforth, to live unto Him"? There are people in the visible church today who have a certain intellectual understanding of the atonement and of the doctrine of justification by faith, but who do not want to obey the Scriptures. They want salvation by grace alone, through faith alone, but they do not want to hear about law or commandments. Today there is much talk about "love" as a kind of replacement for the commandments. "We don't need rules anymore," they say, "not under the New Testament. Now all we need is love, and if you are sure you are acting in love, then that makes it right." It is even said by some today that a "loving" adulterous relationship might be all right, or that homosexual "love" may be quite proper for some people.

Very different indeed is the teaching of the Catechism. How do we really know for sure that something is good? To this question there are only two answers. One answer is that man himself can define what is good and what is right. The other answer is that God alone defines right and wrong. Have we not seen all along in our study of the Catechism which of these is the correct answer? Was the fall of man not precisely this: man trying to determine truth and righteousness for himself? All the way through the gospel accounts we see how Christ answered this question. When the Devil tempted him, Jesus replied, *"It is written"* (Matt. 4:1–11). When he was in conflict with the scribes and Pharisees, he said that they had made the Word of God of no effect by means of their own tradition (Mark 7:13). This was one of the great issues at the time of the Protestant Reformation. Did the church have the right to make laws for itself, or did this right belong only to God? The Church of Rome said that this right belonged to both God and the church. It said that there are two sources of truth: Scripture and tradition. But the Reformers said, "No, there is only one legitimate lawgiver, and that is the Lord." They therefore held to the written Word of God as the only rule of faith and practice. It would be wonderful to be able to say that Protestant churches have remained faithful to this principle, but this is not the case. Even in Reformed churches there is much that is done today with the thought that it is good to do so, even though it is not really in accordance with the Bible.

In order to do what God wants us to do, we need to know three things: first, that we are acting out of faith; second, that we are doing what God tells us to do in his Word; and third, that we are doing what we do for his glory. As an example of the first requirement, suppose that a man actually does what God wants him to for no other reason than that others are doing it. Here is a man, let us say, who is putting ten dollars in the offering plate. He is doing it for one reason: he wants other people to think well of him. The man next to him may give ten dollars also, but for a very different reason. He may do it because he believes in Christ and therefore wants to obey the Word of God. Is it not clear that the "gift" of the first man, though outwardly the same as that of the second man, is really an insult to God?

With regard to the second requirement, suppose a young woman makes a vow of perpetual chastity as a nun. This act may be very highly praised by human wisdom. We can even grant that such a person might do this with sincerity. But that does not make it right. When we read in the Bible that marriage is a God-given option for all of us, and that the doctrine of mandatory celibacy is demonic (1 Tim. 4:1–3), then we begin to see that taking a vow of celibacy is by no means a righteous act. When they came to realize this, the Reformers repudiated such vows of perpetual celibacy and availed themselves of the God-given right to marriage.

Thirdly, it is possible to do something out of faith that is right in itself, and still not do the will of God in the fullest sense. For example, there were some men in Paul's time who preached Christ, but did so out of contention. Their motive was to undercut the influence of Paul. Now they may well have been men who believed in Christ as the Messiah. They certainly preached him as such (and therefore Paul could rejoice in this aspect of what they were doing). Yet because their motive was so unworthy, they were certainly not doing the will of God fully. Paul says that we should do everything for the glory of God (1 Cor. 10:31).

We must have all three of these aspects in view in order to really serve God. And the man who is really renewed will begin to do just that. Because he is a new creature, he does not want to "do his own thing" anymore. No, he believes in the Lord Jesus Christ. Jesus is his Lord (and that means, among other things, that Jesus is in charge) as well as his Savior. And so, because of the incredible thing that Christ did for him, he wants to do what Jesus tells him to do in the Bible. And that leads us directly into the next section of the Heidelberg Catechism, because the Ten Commandments are a brief summary of the Lord's will for his people.

QUESTIONS ON THE LESSON

1. Why is it necessary for us to be converted?
2. What are the two aspects of conversion?
3. How can one be sure of his own conversion?

4. What is the difference between the concept of "love" that is popular today and the biblical concept?
5. What three things are needed in order for us to do what God wants us to do?

QUESTIONS FOR STUDY AND DISCUSSION

1. Is conversion a one-time matter or a continuous process?
2. Is love taught in the Old Testament? Why do so many people have the idea that the New Testament teaches love and the Old Testament teaches law?
3. In the world wars, millions of men took up arms to kill the enemy. Was that an act of love? How do you decide whether it was or not in any particular case?

Lord's Day 34

SCRIPTURE READINGS: *Exodus 20:1–17;*
Matthew 22:37–40; Mark 12:30

92. **Q. What is the law of God?**

A. God spake all these words, saying: *I am Jehovah thy God,
who brought thee out of the land of Egypt, out of the house of
bondage.*

    I. *Thou shalt have no other gods before me.*

    II. *Thou shalt not make unto thee a graven image, nor any
likeness of any thing that is in heaven above, or that is
in the earth beneath, or that is in the water under the
earth; thou shalt not bow down thyself unto them, nor
serve them; for I Jehovah thy God am a jealous God,
visiting the iniquity of the fathers upon the children,
upon the third and upon the fourth generation of them
that hate me, and showing lovingkindness unto thousands of them that love me and keep my commandments.*

    III. *Thou shalt not take the name of Jehovah thy God in vain:
for Jehovah will not hold him guiltless that taketh his name
in vain.*

    IV. *Remember the sabbath day, to keep it holy. Six days shalt
thou labor, and do all thy work; but the seventh day is a
sabbath unto Jehovah thy God: in it thou shalt not do
any work, thou, nor thy son, nor thy daughter, thy man-
servant, nor thy maid-servant, nor thy cattle, nor thy*

stranger that is within thy gates: for in six days Jehovah made heaven and earth, the sea, and all that in them is, and rested the seventh day: wherefore Jehovah blessed the sabbath day, and hallowed it.

V. *Honor thy father and thy mother, that thy days may be long in the land which Jehovah thy God giveth thee.*

VI. *Thou shalt not kill.*

VII. *Thou shalt not commit adultery.*

VIII. *Thou shalt not steal.*

IX. *Thou shalt not bear false witness against thy neighbor.*

X. *Thou shalt not covet thy neighbor's house, thou shalt not covet thy neighbor's wife, nor his man-servant, nor his maid-servant, nor his ox, nor his ass, nor anything that is thy neighbor's.*

93. Q. How are these commandments divided?

A. Into two tables; the first of which teaches what must be our attitude toward God; the second, what duties we owe to our neighbor.

Two things are worthy of our attention at this point in the teaching of the Heidelberg Catechism. First, the authors of the Catechism regard the Ten Commandments as a summary of God's will for the Christian. This was clearly seen in Answers 90 and 91. There we learned that when we become new creatures in Christ, we "delight to live according to the will of God in all good works." But "good works" are then defined as things that are done "according to the law of God." So it is quite clear that the Ten Commandments (which immediately follow this definition) are God's own summary of his holy will for us. Thus, the attempt—which has been made even by some who claim to be Reformed—to deny the abiding relevance and binding character of one or another of the Ten Commandments is contrary to the teaching of the Catechism. The commandment that has been called into question most often in recent times is the fourth commandment. And it is true that the Catechism does not say as much about this commandment as does the Westminster Confession of Faith (or the Larger and Shorter Catechisms). This does not, however, justify the allegation that we are free to take a lax view of this commandment. This is wholly inconsistent, not only with the inclusion of this law in the summary of what God's will is for the Christian, but also with the remarkable statement (which we will deal with in greater detail later) in Answer 115! If no one in this life is able to obey the Ten Commandments perfectly, Question 115 asks, "why, then, will God have the ten commandments preached so strictly?" The answer is very significant. The Catechism says that this is needed so that "we may learn more and more to know our sinful nature, and so become the more earnest in seeking remission of sins and righteousness in Christ" and, at the same time, "constantly endeavor" to reach "the goal of perfection." The Catechism thus declares that this principle applies to the fourth commandment too, which would not be true if it had been abrogated or relaxed. The modern attempt to weaken the high demands of the fourth commandment does not square with the Heidelberg Catechism.

The second thing deserving comment here is the statement in Answer 93 that the Ten Commandments are divided into two tables. This is the traditional view, and it is deduced from the following scriptural data. First, the Bible says that the Lord gave Moses *two tablets of the Testimony*" on Mount Sinai (Ex. 31:18). We are not told, however, what was written on the one or the other of these two tablets. Second, Christ summed up the law in *two* statements: we are to love God with all our heart, soul, mind, and strength, and we are to love our neighbor as ourselves (Mark 12:30). This might seem to suggest the traditional division. It must be understood, however, that the traditional view—useful as it is—is not the only possible way of putting the matter. It may be—as some scholars have suggested—that the whole law was written on each of the two tables of stone given to Moses. This seems to be in accord with the customs of that day in the making of covenants. It is also true that every one of these Ten Commandments has something to do with our relationship to God. For example, since Paul says that covetousness is idolatry (Eph. 5:5), the tenth commandment clearly does not teach us merely "what duties we owe to our neighbor." It can also be questioned—even if one does make a division into a first and a second table—whether the division should be made between the fourth and fifth commandments. The fifth commandment deals with the whole sphere of duly constituted authority. But there is no authority except that which comes from God. It is for this reason that children are commanded to obey their parents "in the Lord." In other words, obedience to duly constituted authority is not only "what duties we owe to our neighbor" but also an expression of our obedience to God himself.

It must be remembered that all creeds and confessions are fallible. Unlike the Bible, which is inerrant, the Reformed confessions (as they, themselves, teach us) must always be tested, again and again, by the Scriptures. We can fully and completely agree with the Catechism when it says that the Ten Commandments are the proper and true standard of obedience for the Christian. We can also fully and completely agree that the Ten Commandments teach "what must be our attitude toward God" and "what duties we owe to our neighbor." We are therefore not criticizing the Catechism if we say we are not quite satisfied with the traditional understanding of the structure of the Decalogue as a whole, for the reasons given above. In saying this, however, we want to add an affirmative note. The Catechism *is* correct in making a distinction between what is first and what is second—putting God first and man second. Indeed, it is our conviction that the reason for the particular order that we find in these Ten Commandments is the primacy of God. We would therefore humbly suggest that this part of the Catechism would be improved if it went something like this:

93.   Q. *How are these commandments organized?*
      A. *They focus on the two spheres of life, the first having to do more directly with the worship of God, and the second being what God requires of us in his service.*

There may be a better way of putting it than this. But we believe that this is closer to the intent of the law itself and avoids the arbitrary elements of the traditional view. The following outline of the commandments will indicate what we have in mind.

What Is Required?	The Ten Commandments	What Is Forbidden?
—to know, acknowledge, and worship the true God	1. The **object** of worship: *Have no other gods before my face.*	—to deny or fail to acknowledge God, or to worship a false god
—to worship God as he has commanded	2. The **manner** of worship: *No image or likeness— don't bow down to them.*	—to worship God through images or in any other way not commanded
—to use God's name and ordinances in a reverent manner	3. The **attitude** of worship: *Take not the name of God in vain.*	—to use God's name or ordinances profanely (irreverently)
—to worship one day each week and to work six days	4. The **time** of worship and work: *Remember the Sabbath; six days you shall labor.*	—to observe man-made holy days or to be slothful in daily work
—to honor and obey God-instituted authority (parents, rulers)	5. The rule of **authority**: *Honor your father and mother.*	—to dishonor or disobey God-instituted authority (parents, police)
—to preserve our own lives and the lives of others	6. The rule of **life**: *You shall not murder.*	—to take our own or another's life unjustly
—to preserve our own and our neighbor's chastity	7. The rule of **sex**: *You shall not commit adultery.*	—to engage in sexual immorality in thought, word, or deed
—to advance our own and our neighbor's wealth and possessions	8. The rule of **property:** *You shall not steal.*	—to do anything detrimental to our own or another's wealth or estate
—to promote truth and our own good name and that of others	9. The rule of **speech**: *You shall not bear false witness.*	—to injure the cause of truth or the reputation of ourselves or another
—to be content and to rejoice with others in what they have	10. The rule of **desire**: *You shall not covet.*	—to envy, be discontent, or wish any evil on our neighbor

Before we discuss the various commandments in particular, we need to grasp some of the general principles that apply to all of them. First, there is an order of importance in the arrangement of these commandments. The organizing principle is the centrality—or supremacy—of God. The natural man completely fails to comprehend this. He thinks that he is "not too bad" if he refrains from stealing, murder, and adultery, while paying not the slightest heed to the higher duties of worship! However, the greatest sins of men are in the area of worship.

Second, each commandment teaches both what is required and what is forbidden. Eight of the commandments are put in a negative form: "You shall not . . ." Two are stated positively. But by comparing Scripture with Scripture, we learn that when God gives us the one (either the "shall" or the "shall not"), the other is inevitably implied. (It is there by good and necessary inference).

Third, ten commandments are sufficient. In the Scriptures, the number ten is often used to indicate completeness. When the bridegroom in the Song of Solomon praises ten aspects of his wife's beauty, for example, it is a way of saying "You are perfect." Well, God's Ten Commandments *are* perfect. The Decalogue does not stand in need of any additions.

QUESTIONS ON THE LESSON

1. If we understand that the Ten Commandments are God's own summary of his holy will, two classic errors will be avoided. What are they?
2. What is the traditional way of accounting for the fact that there were two tables of the law?
3. What ancient custom suggests a different explanation?
4. What is the first principle to understand as to the arrangement of the Ten Commandments?
5. What is the second?
6. What is the third?

QUESTIONS FOR STUDY AND DISCUSSION

1. Is it really true that the proper worship of God is more important than our duty to man? Is it more important than not murdering your neighbor? Explain.

2. Do the Ten Commandments fully cover every aspect of our duty in modern life? Where do traffic laws fit into the Ten Commandments?

LORD'S DAY 34—CONTINUED

SCRIPTURE READINGS: 1 John 5:21;
Deuteronomy 18:9–10; Acts 5:29

94. Q. What does God require in the first commandment?

A. That, as much as I love my soul's salvation, I avoid and flee all idolatry, sorcery, soothsaying, superstition, invocation of saints or other creatures; and that I rightly acknowledge the only true God, trust in Him alone, submit to Him with all humility and patience, expect all good from Him only, and love, fear, and honor Him with my whole heart; so that I leave and forsake all creatures rather than do even the least thing against His will.

95. Q. What is idolatry?

A. It is, instead of the one true God who has revealed Himself in His Word, or besides Him, to devise or have something else on which to place our trust.

Idolatry is the ultimate sin. It is also, in a sense, the root of all other sins. We see this clearly in Colossians 3:5, where the apostle Paul says that *"covetousness . . . is idolatry"* (emphasis added). If we even begin to desire what God forbids, we are already—in effect —renouncing the true God as our God. We are saying in effect, "I don't like God the way he is, as he is revealed in the Bible. I want God to be different. I want a different God—a God who doesn't make these demands on me that I find distasteful." It was no doubt for this reason that the apostle John gave this warning to believers in the early church: *"Keep yourselves from idols"* (1 John 5:21).

Idolatry is the substitution of a false god in place of the true God. It can come to expression in many ways. In Old Testament times it often came to expression in the production and use of visible statues. Dagon (1 Sam. 5), for example, was the god of the Philistines. Some have thought that this idol had the appearance partly of a fish and partly of a man, but this is not certain. But it did have a head, arms, and hands. More recent scholarship suggests that Dagon was a fertility god, the god of the grain harvest. But, be that as it may, the key point is perfectly clear. Dagon was *created by man*. Dagon was not a legitimate representation of the true God, but a false projection of the sinful minds of men, creating a god in preference to the true God.

A false god can be created in other ways than by constructing a statue. We have much the same thing in much of modern theology. Man sets himself up as the judge of the Bible. He decides, with his human wisdom, that the Bible has primitive ideas about God, which we have now outgrown. In place of these primitive ideas, he insists, we now have a much higher concept of a God through the teaching of Jesus. And what is this much higher concept? Well, it is the idea that God is a god of love, a god who loves everybody so much that there is no need to fear any such thing as hell and damnation. This, of course, is the very briefest attempt at a summary. But it shows how modern man creates his own god using doctrinal formulations, just as truly as the ancient Philistine did it using wood and stone. But whatever man invents to replace the true God of the Bible, it is, by that very fact, an idol.

And that is not all. Even if a man attempts to serve both God and someone (or something) else, that is still idolatry. Jesus said that no one can serve both God and mammon (meaning "wealth" or "riches") (Matt. 6:24). The true God demands exclusive devotion. He is our Creator and we are his creatures. He therefore has a perfect right to our exclusive devotion. This is doubly true for us as Christians. We are his not only because of our creation but also because of our redemption. Christ bought us back, as it were, from Satan's dominion, so that we could again belong to God as his children. When we see this clearly, we will realize how wicked it is to be devoted to anyone (or anything) instead of, or even along with, the true God.

Therefore, the Catechism quite properly stresses both the negative and the positive requirements of the first commandment. On the negative side, we must shun practices that compromise the absolute claims of God on us. Superstition originally meant any "worship over and above that which was appointed by proper authority." When the Catechism was written, it meant "the observance of unnecessary and uncommanded rites and practices in religion" ("Superstition," John McClintock and James Strong, *Cyclopaedia of Biblical, Theological, and Ecclesiastical Literature,* vol. 10, p. 33). To avoid superstition, we must be sure that our concept of God, and our practices that express it, are in accord with God's self-revelation in the Scriptures.

Thus, on the positive side, we must acknowledge the true God. We must come to know him, in other words, as he really is. And we can do this only as we pay close heed to the revelation that he has given us in the Bible. And what does the true God, who has revealed himself in the Bible, require? He requires that we love him with *all* our heart, soul, mind, and strength (Mark 12:30). He requires that we worship and serve Him *only* (Matt. 4:10). This means that we must, quite literally, be willing to forsake anything (Matt. 9:6ff.) or anyone (Luke 4:26) in order to worship and serve him only.

To put it quite bluntly, then: true religion is totalitarian. In this modern era we have seen much totalitarianism in which some man (Hitler, Stalin) or some ideology of man (fascism, communism) has made dictatorial claims on every aspect of man's life. Over against this human totalitarianism is divine totalitarianism. God and his Christ demand absolute allegiance, and they demand it in every sphere of life. We must see to it that our children are educated his way, not the false way dictated by humanism. We must also insist on our right to live by God's law in business, in politics, and so on. When the humanist says that our religion must be excluded from the spheres of education, business, politics, and the like, we must refuse to bow down to the humanly devised gods he sets up over these areas of life.

Let us take a particular example. Suppose you are a teacher in a public school. The state says, "In this business of education, the state is god. So you are not allowed to teach that man was created by the God of the Bible. You must teach that man is a product of time plus chance (or accident). In this area you must bow down to the state, and acknowledge the state as your god." The Christian must reply, "No, I *cannot* and I *will not* do this." Instead, he must dare to teach that evolution is false and that Jehovah did create man. Why? Because he knows (as the Catechism so rightly says) that the very first commandment in the law of God requires him to "leave and forsake all creatures rather than do even the least thing against His will." Of course, this will not be easy. But it is right, and that is what counts.

QUESTIONS ON THE LESSON

1. What is idolatry?
2. Is an idol made out of wood or stone the only kind of idol?
3. What does it mean to serve both God and mammon?
4. Why is it impossible to serve both?
5. Why does this commandment impose a form of totalitarian authority upon us?

QUESTIONS FOR STUDY AND DISCUSSION

1. Do Roman Catholics still pray to saints today? For what reasons?
2. What gods are commonly served and worshiped today in Western countries?
3. Choose two other commandments and explain how breaking them also involves the transgression of the first commandment.
4. Is it possible to teach in a state school without compromising on the truth? Explain your answer and give some examples.

LORD's DAY 35

SCRIPTURE READINGS: *Exodus 20:22–26;*
Acts 17:29; John 4:22–24

96. **Q. What does God require in the second commandment?**
    A. That we in no wise make any image of God, nor worship Him in any other way than He has commanded in His Word.

97. **Q. May we, then, not make any image at all?**
    A. God neither can nor may be visibly represented in any way. As for creatures, though they may be visibly represented, yet God forbids us to make or have any likeness of them in order to worship them or serve God by them.

98. **Q. But may not images be tolerated in the churches as books for the laity?**
    A. No; for we must not be wiser than God, who will not have His people taught by dumb images, but by the living preaching of His Word.

The second commandment forbids the manufacture or use of any statue or picture purporting to represent God. Yet how common it is today for Christians to do both. At the time of the Reformation, this forbidden practice was deeply ingrained in Roman Catholic thinking and practice. Today it is almost as common among Protestants as it is among Catholics. Why? The main reason seems to be that Jesus Christ is thought of, not as God, but as a mere man. It is perfectly true, of course, that Jesus Christ was and is human. But he may not be *defined* in terms of his humanity. No, Christ is (and was and ever shall be) a divine person, the second person of the Godhead. In the fullness of time he took unto his divine person a human nature, so that he is now both divine and human. Because of his divinity, it is not proper to make any likenesses of Jesus (whether a statue or a portrait). If it be argued that it would be wrong to make any representation of the divine Christ, but that it is all right to make such of the human Jesus, the answer is simple. It is a heresy (called Nestorianism) to divide the two natures of Christ. The only true Christ *is* divine, and his deity cannot be separated from his humanity. Therefore, it is wrong to make representations of him. John Calvin was right when he said that he wanted no pictures of Christ other than those authorized by God in the Bible. The only representations that he found authorized in the Bible were in baptism and the Lord's Supper!

Observe, however, that the Catechism *does* allow for the making of statues and pictures of mere men, when they are not made as aids to worship. Some Christian groups have not been willing to allow this. Some Mennonites, for instance, have even refused to be photographed, because they understand the second commandment to forbid representations of any kind whatsoever. Why, then, does the Catechism allow them? The answer is that in the context of the first, third, and fourth commandments, the second one is concerned with the proper worship of the true God. If the first commandment informs us as to the proper *object* of worship, the second commandment directs us to the proper *manner*. It does not, therefore, deal with many other questions, such as the question of what is proper in the production of money. In our Lord's day, the likeness of Caesar was found on coins (Luke 20:24). But Jesus did not denounce the use of these coins, or refuse to use them. From this we can see that it is quite proper for a nation to honor its great leaders with statues, likenesses on coins, and the like. Such things are not a violation of the second commandment as long as there is no intention to worship them or to worship God through them.

But it is precisely such an intention that has brought images and pictures back into many Protestant churches. One of the oldest arguments for the use of statues and pictures of Jesus and the saints is that they are needed for instruction. Indeed, this is the principal reason why it is so difficult today to find Sunday school materials that are not full of such pictures. Yet the Catechism rightly teaches that these should be rejected because God "will not have His people taught by dumb images." The proper means of instruction is the Word of God alone, because it alone is God's own revelation. This does not mean that a Sunday school teacher may never use any teaching aids whatsoever. There is no reason at all, for instance, why a teacher may not use a good map, or a photograph of the Sea of Galilee or of some artifact from the time of Christ. All of these things can be extremely useful, and they are perfectly proper for the simple reason that they do not attempt to add anything to God's revelation out of man's imagination. And that is the real issue at stake in the second commandment.

How are we to worship the true God? To that question there are but two possible answers. One answer is, "We will worship God as *he* directs, because then we will know that what we are doing is pleasing to him." The other answer is, "We will worship God as *we* please, even though he has not authorized us to do this." It is evident, right here, that there is a very close relationship between the first two commandments. The Roman Catholic and Lutheran churches do not even make a distinction between the first two commandments. They include the second commandment as a part of the first. This would not be so bad if they did justice to what Exodus 20:4–6 says. But they do not. That is why Roman Catholic and Lutheran churches see nothing wrong with statues or pictures of Jesus (and the saints) in their churches. Our Reformed fathers, on the other hand, correctly saw that the second commandment safeguards against a falling away from the first. That is, we begin to depart from the true God the moment we begin to rely on our own imagination (thinking up our own idea of God) rather than God's revelation (which is complete in the Bible).

The commandment speaks in terms of a particular, concrete example. It speaks of the specific sin of making a graven image or likeness for religious purposes, a sin which was very common in Moses' day. But the Catechism quite rightly sees in this commandment a general principle of much wider application. The principle is that we must not worship God "in any other way than He has commanded in His Word." It was on the basis of this principle, for example, that the Reformed churches rejected five additional rituals that Rome called sacraments. They were rejected because they were not commanded by God and were an expression of man's own imagination. For the same reason, Calvin and others in the Reformed churches rejected Christmas, Good Friday, and Easter as special holy days. Since the Lord himself had not appointed any such days in his Word, there was no legitimate basis for them. If we stop and think about it, it will be all too evident how far the Reformed churches have fallen from their own profession.

QUESTIONS ON THE LESSON

1. Why is it that so many Protestants now make and use various representations of God the Son?
2. Why is it wrong to do this?
3. Why does the Catechism allow us to make representations of men such as George Washington or Winston Churchill?
4. What are the two possible ways of worshiping God?
5. Why have the Roman Catholics and Lutherans ignored what this commandment actually says?
6. How do we know that this commandment applies to other man-made inventions in worship, and not only to pictures and images?

QUESTIONS FOR STUDY AND DISCUSSION

1. Discuss the practice of portraying a scene such as the feeding of the five thousand by showing the crowd with Jesus' back turned as he gives the food to his disciples. Would such a picture violate this commandment? Why or why not?
2. There are several occasions in Scripture in which dancing was done to praise the Lord. Is this a reason to include dancing in our worship?
3. List several worship practices that are common in Protestant churches but are not commanded or warranted by God in Scripture.

LORD'S DAYS 36 AND 37

SCRIPTURE READINGS: *Ecclesiastes 5:1–7;*
Matthew 5:33–37; 10:32–33

99. **Q. What is required in the third commandment?**
A. That we must not by cursing or perjury, nor by unnecessary swearing, profane or abuse the Name of God, nor by
our silence or connivance become partakers of these horrible sins in others; and briefly, that we use the holy Name
of God no otherwise than with fear and reverence, to the
end that He may be rightly confessed and worshipped by
us, and be glorified in all our words and works.

100. **Q. Is, then, the profaning of God's Name by swearing and
cursing so heinous a sin that His wrath is kindled even
against those who do not, as much as in them lies, help
to prevent and to forbid such cursing and swearing?**
A. Certainly; for no sin is greater or more provoking to God
than the profaning of His Name; wherefore, also, He has
commanded this sin to be punished with death.

101. **Q. But may we not swear by the Name of God in a godly
manner?**
A. Yes; when the magistrate demands it of his subjects, or
when otherwise necessity requires us thus to confirm fidelity and truth, for the glory of God and the welfare of
our neighbor; for such swearing is grounded in God's Word,
and therefore was rightly used by the saints in the Old and
the New Testament.

102. Q. May we also swear by saints or any other creatures?
   A. No; for a lawful oath is a calling upon God, as the only
      Searcher of hearts, to bear witness to the truth, and to pun-
      ish me if I swear falsely; which honor is due to no crea-
      ture.

It is important to see this commandment in the light of the first two.
In the first commandment we learn that the true God alone is the proper
object of worship. In the second we learn what the proper *manner* of worship is (namely, only what God has commanded). In this commandment
we learn the proper *attitude* of worship.

To "take" God's name means, centrally, to become a Christian. A
woman "takes" her husband's name when she takes her marriage vows.
By these vows she promises exclusive commitment to her husband. If,
however, she is then unfaithful and breaks the marriage covenant, she
has taken her husband's name in vain. In a similar way, we profess our
faith in Jesus Christ and are privileged to be called Christians. But if
we are not sincere and become covenant breakers, we have "taken his
name in vain." The form is there, in other words, but the reality is not.
We say the right thing, but we do not really mean it. It is for this reason that wise Solomon warned us not to be careless when we *go to the
house of God* or *"utter anything hastily before God"* (Eccl. 5:1–2). As a
matter of fact, *"It is better not to vow than to vow and not pay* [or fulfill
our vow]" (v. 5).

We make a big mistake, then, if we think of this commandment
only—or even mainly—in terms of the vile language that we often hear
coming out of the mouths of those who do not profess to be Christians.
It is true, of course, that we ought to "use the holy Name of God" with
reverence. No one has a right to speak the name that is above every
name without an inner sense of awe and worship. So it is certainly true
that this commandment is broken by the evil habit of swearing that is
so common today. But even so, it is the Christian who bears the primary responsibility. We should expect the ungodly to curse and to use
unnecessary oaths. But the Catechism quite properly puts the focus on
us by saying that we must not "by our silence or connivance become
partakers of these horrible sins in others."

There are those who profess faith in Jesus. Yet they can hear his
name used in curses all day long and do or say nothing about it. It is
not so with those who truly reverence his name. They just can't stand

it when his name is constantly treated with disrespect. That is why they cannot and will not be silent. For example, I once drove some distance to see an item advertised in a want ad. In talking to the man who was selling the item, the opportunity came up to mention the Christian faith. Then came a very pleasant surprise. The man indicated that he was not a Christian himself, but that he had been very impressed, shortly before that, by a certain man who did something unusual. When a group of workers began to tell dirty jokes and use the Lord's name in vain, this man had refused to be a silent bystander. Instead, he had simply turned, the moment he heard what was being said, and walked away. This man, who was not a Christian, had seen him do it. And he said, "I'm sure he was a Christian." He was right. That man was indeed a Christian. As a matter of fact, he happened to be a member of our church. And because of his silent protest against taking the Lord's name in vain, people knew that he was a genuine Christian.

But why, it may be asked, does God include such an awesome warning as a part of this commandment? Is it not because of the danger of a superficial, purely external religion? Suppose, for instance, that I belong to a Reformed church. Does this not mean that every Lord's Day the true God is worshiped? Can we not also say that this is a faithful church, and that the true God is therefore worshiped in a proper manner—as he has commanded? Yes, but right here is a danger. It is the danger that I might say—because of these things—"All is well with my soul!" I might even boast, saying, "We worship the true God, and we do it in the right manner." Ah yes, but is my heart really in it? Do I really "use the holy Name of God . . . with fear and reverence"? If I do not do so, then in spite of these things God will not be pleased with my worship. That is why this momentous warning of judgment comes at this point. It comes because all of us who confess ourselves to be Christians need to remember that "our heart must be in it."

This must be the sense of the third commandment. Otherwise, who could be saved? Could the apostle Peter? The Bible says that he denied Jesus with curses. Yet we know that Peter's sin was forgiven. We see, then, that the warning contained in this commandment does not mean that a man will necessarily be damned forever if he has ever taken the Lord's name in vain. No, if such a man repents of his sin and turns to the Lord, he will surely be forgiven (as Peter was). But the man who professes repentance and faith, but does not depart from iniquity, is the one who will be rejected (Matt. 7:21–23). This is exactly what deforms the Christian church so badly today. In churches all across the world there are people who profess the name of Jesus and then live just as they please. They do not tremble at his Word. They do not keep his Sabbath. They do not respect the lawful authority of the church elders. And we could go on. But there is no need. It is this great sin that the third commandment is concerned with. God hates nothing so much as hypocrisy. And what is hypocrisy? It is the wearing of a false mask. It is claiming to be in submission to Jesus Christ as Lord, while not really being in submission at all. And what could deserve the wrath of God more richly than that?

In our Lord's great Sermon on the Mount, there is a section that is often misunderstood. It is misunderstood because it is taken out of context. The context is our Lord's careful series of contrasts between the false traditions of the scribes and Pharisees, on the one hand, and the true meaning of Scripture, on the other. When Jesus said *"You have heard that it was said"* (Matt. 5:21, 27, 33, 38, 43), he did not mean the same thing as when he said *"It is written."* To the contrary, the thing that people had heard was the false interpretation, then current, which Jesus was combating. According to this wrong tradition, there were two kinds of oaths (and vows). In the one, a man would actually pronounce the name of Jehovah. When he did that—according to this tradition— he had to keep his oath. But in the other kind of oath, a man could avoid the use of Jehovah's name by using an expression such as "his footstool" or "the city of Jerusalem." He could say "I swear by holy Jerusalem," and when he did that, they said he was not bound in the way he would be if he used Jehovah's name directly. So it became a widespread practice to use this second kind of vow. But why, we may ask, would people do this? Why would they swear by the temple or the city of Jerusalem? The answer is quite simple: they wanted the "cash value" of an oath or vow without the liability that goes with it. They wanted the benefits, in other words, without risking the penalties. And Jesus recognized this sham for what it really was: a species of hypocrisy. That is why he says, in this context, *"But I say to you, do not swear at all. . . . But let your 'Yes' be 'Yes,' and your 'No,' 'No.' For whatever is more than these is from the evil one"* (Matt. 5:34, 37). He did not mean that it is always wrong to take an oath, or make a vow. We know this because he did not come to abolish the law of God (Matt. 5:17), and oaths and vows are commanded in the law (Deut. 10:20). We also know it because our Lord himself answered the high priest under oath (see

Num. 5:9 and Matt. 26:63). And, of course, the apostles who knew the mind of our Lord did likewise (see 2 Cor. 1:23).

If the whole world were truly Christian, there would be no need for oaths or vows. And to the extent that we are able to do so, Christians should strive to live without recourse to them. What this means is that, for a real Christian, a simple yes or no should carry such integrity and sincerity that it will be sufficient. Indeed, this ought to be the hallmark of a genuine Christian community: whatever these people say is dependable. Yet because the world is evil, there is—and until Christ comes again, there will be—a need for oaths and vows. Jesus did not say that oaths and vows themselves *are* evil. He said only that they *come from* (the prevalence of) evil. In a court of law, for instance, it is still necessary that people be put on oath. In this way sinners are temporarily reminded that they will be judged for what they say, and this does reduce the amount of exaggeration, distortion, and perjury. There is also a need for vows in marriage and for membership vows in the church. And when these are imposed by duly constituted authority (that is, persons with God-given authority in church or state), they ought not to be rejected by God's people.

When the Catechism was written, a situation prevailed in the Roman Catholic Church that was not unlike what our Lord condemned in his Sermon on the Mount. People would swear by St. Jude or by the virgin Mary. Here again, because these "saints" were thought of as being close to God, the "cash value" of the oath was felt to be almost as great as if one swore by the name of Jesus. Perhaps it was also thought that in this way one could avoid the heavy penalty for swearing falsely that would necessarily accompany the use of God's name. In any event, it is utterly wrong (as Jesus made clear in Matt. 5:34–35) to swear by any other name than that of the true God. This is so because the idea of a vow is this: we call upon God to judge us according to the sincerity and integrity of what we are saying. Since such searching judgment belongs to God alone, it is a great sin to swear by any mere creature.

The third commandment contains an awesome warning. It is so momentous, in fact, that some have thought it best to vow nothing at all rather than risk this threatened judgment. For example, I have known of covenant children who, because they are afraid of not being able to live up to the required vows, try to "play it safe" by holding back from making a public profession. But this is not the answer. Every commandment that forbids something also, by implication, commands something. The opposite of "taking God's name in vain" is not a refusal to take God's name at all. No, it is rather to "take God's name in sincerity and truth." It is only the man who does this who will be clear of God's wrath announced in this third commandment.

Questions on the Lesson

1. What does it mean to take God's name?
2. What does the example of Peter prove with respect to the warning stated in this commandment?
3. In the Sermon on the Mount, what was Jesus referring to when he said, "You have heard that it was said"?
4. How do we know that the teaching of Jesus was not intended to absolutely forbid all swearing?
5. Is it ever our duty to swear?

Questions for Study and Discussion

1. What religious groups forbid any taking of oaths or making of vows? What basis do they claim for their practice?
2. What different types of bad language can you think of? Are all these types always wrong for the Christian to use? Would it ever be right for a Christian to use a "four-letter word"?
3. In what situations should you speak out against blasphemy? Would you have a right to tell your employer not to blaspheme?
4. Since a Christian may not use blasphemous or immoral speech, how can he add strong emphasis to his speech when it is needed?

LORD'S DAY 38

SCRIPTURE READINGS: *Hebrews 4:1–10;*
Acts 20:1–16; 1 Corinthians 16:2; Revelation 1:10

103. Q. What does God require in the fourth commandment?

  A. First, that the ministry of the gospel and the schools be
  maintained; and that I, especially on the Sabbath, that is,
  the day of rest, diligently attend the church of God, to
  learn God's Word, to use the sacraments, to call publicly
  upon the Lord, and to give Christian alms. Second, that
  all the days of my life I rest from my evil works, let the
  Lord work in me by His Holy Spirit, and thus begin in this
  life the eternal Sabbath.

When the Heidelberg Catechism was written, there was no doubt
about one thing: God gave us *ten* commandments. It is true that there
is an element of ambiguity in the writings of some of the great Reformers with respect to the fourth commandment. Calvin himself
seems, at one time, to argue against continuity between the Old Testament Sabbath and the New Testament Lord's Day, and then, at another time, to argue for it. There was a similar ambiguity evident at
the great Synod of Dordt. It held, on the one hand, that there is a
temporary, ceremonial aspect to the fourth commandment, and yet, on
the other hand, that there is also a permanent moral element. From
that day to this there has been some disagreement with respect to this
matter.

Six points were adopted by the Synod of Dordt (1618–19). They
are as follows (as quoted from Idzerd Van Dellen and Martin Monsma,
The Church Order Commentary, p. 276):

1. In the fourth commandment of God's Law there is a cere-
    monial and a moral element.
2. The rest on the seventh day after the creation, and the strict
    observance of this day with which the Jewish people were
    charged particularly, was ceremonial.
3. That a definite and appointed day has been set aside to the
    service of God, and that for this purpose as much rest is re-
    quired as is necessary for the service of God and for hallowed
    contemplation, this element is moral.
4. The Sabbath of the Jews having been set aside, Christians are
    in duty bound to hallow the Day of the Lord solemnly.
5. This day has always been kept in the early Church since the
    time of the Apostles.
6. This day must be so consecrated unto the service of God that
    upon it men rest from all servile labors, except those required
    by charity and present necessities, and likewise from all such
    recreations as prevent the service of God.

With all due respect to this great Synod, we are nevertheless convinced
that their formulation does not state the matter perfectly. We find nothing ceremonial in the fourth commandment itself. What it does is to
prescribe a seven-day cycle with a proportional division. Out of every
seven-day cycle six days are to be given over to what we would call our
routine activities. Then, out of that same cycle of seven days, one day
is to be given over to rest and worship. It is certainly true that the Jews
were required to observe the last day of the weekly cycle. But we learn
this from other places in Scripture, not from the commandment itself.
It is also true that the Old Testament Sabbath (our Saturday) has been
set aside (Col. 2:6). Why, then, are Christians "in duty bound to hallow the Day of the Lord solemnly"? The answer is: because of the fourth
commandment and the clear New Testament teaching that the first day
(the Lord's Day) has now been designated for rest and worship out of
each weekly cycle.

   The word *Sabbath* means "cessation." When God first rested (or
"sabbathed") after the six days of creation, the Sabbath, as a day of rest,
was instituted (Gen. 2:1–2). However, because of the fall of man, there
had to be a new creation. God sent his Son Jesus to do the great work
necessary for us to be saved. When Jesus completed his work, he also
entered his rest (or Sabbath), just as God did after the first creation was

finished (Heb. 4:10). This being the case, we see no reason at all for saying that the fourth commandment *itself* contains anything ceremonial. We also believe there is just as much reason now, as in the past, for taking a strict view of this commandment. (Is this not exactly what the Catechism itself teaches us a bit later on? Does it not remind us that we should not even have a single "inclination or thought contrary to any of God's commandments" [Answer 113], and that God wants *all* of these laws to be taught "strictly" [Answer 115]?)

Three things remain to be said about this section of the Catechism. First, it quite rightly puts the primary emphasis on the joyous character of the Lord's Day. We come together on this sacred day to celebrate an accomplished redemption. How could anyone understand what this really means without being festive? Second, for this very reason the emphasis falls on the gathering together of the Lord's people to hear the official proclamation of the good news and to learn its profound lessons even more deeply. Understanding more of the height and depth and length and breadth, as it were, of God's great work of redemption demands no less than a diligent use of the means of grace every Lord's Day. Third, to the Heidelberg Catechism belongs the honor of seeing what is, after all, the capstone of the significance of the fourth commandment. The Sabbath is the sign of the people of God all the way through the history of salvation. It was set there, in the beginning, to mark the work of creation. It also looks forward to the great day of perfected fellowship in the Lord's immediate presence. The present Lord's Day, then, must be lived out in terms of this wonderful tension between the "already" and the "not yet." We are not yet there in the eternal Sabbath rest in the kingdom of glory. But we are already there in a sense when we come together faithfully on the weekly Sabbath.

Some people today do not like to hear that we should keep the Sabbath strictly. But we should. This does not mean that we should do it grudgingly. It does not mean that we should find it a burden. No, what it means is that we should see it as a delight, and yet realize at the same time, as the Synod of Dordt so rightly said, that we "are in duty bound to hallow the Day of the Lord solemnly" (though, at the same time, in a festive manner). One thing is sure: no one will ever get the natural man to put these things together. The only thing that can ever bring a man to do it is God's transforming work within his heart, making him a part of his new creation and thereby making him a partaker of the eternal Sabbath. Can you honestly say that this is your heart's desire?

Questions on the Lesson

1. Is there a ceremonial element in the fourth commandment?
2. In what way is the word *seventh* commonly misunderstood?
3. Is there a contradiction between saying that we must keep this day strictly and saying that we should do it in a festive way?
4. If the Sabbath is a "sign" of the people of God, what does that say about this present generation?
5. What is necessary before we can really keep the Sabbath?

Questions for Study and Discussion

1. Does God desire that we keep the Sabbath strictly?
2. What inferences about the change to worshiping on the first day of the week can be drawn from the account in Acts 20:1–16?
3. What differences can you find between the Heidelberg Catechism and the Westminster Confession of Faith regarding the Sabbath? Do you think their positions are contradictory?

LORD'S DAY 39

SCRIPTURE READINGS: *Ephesians 6:1–9; Romans 13:1–7*

104. Q. What does God require in the fifth commandment?

A. That I show all honor, love, and fidelity to my father and mother, and to all in authority over me; submit myself with due obedience to their good instruction and correction; and also bear patiently with their weaknesses and shortcomings, since it pleases God to govern us by their hand.

Back in the 1960s we saw a very interesting phenomenon. All over the Western world young people turned against the value system of their parents. Popular music became a driving force with many. There was also experimentation with drugs. Then came what many called the greatest "trip" of all—the Jesus trip. We saw religious communes and cults. Many began to call themselves "Jesus freaks." They said they were "turned on" to Jesus. Yet in truth, it would be hard to think of anything more distant from the Jesus of Scripture.

The Bible tells us that Jesus was *"without sin"* (Heb. 4:15), even though he was truly human (Heb. 2:4). We also know that Mary and Joseph were imperfect parents to Jesus (Luke 1:47; Rom. 5:2). If ever there was a case, in other words, where it might have been plausibly argued that a child had the right to go against parental authority, it was in the case of Jesus. Yet Jesus did not rebel. To the contrary, he remained subject to his parents until he was about thirty years of age (Luke 3:23). He did so because he understood that he too was born under the law of God (Gal. 4:4), and that this law required due submission to parental authority. When he finally did leave home, it was in response to the call of God to do his work as the Messiah.

Now the thing that strikes us, all the way through the New Testament account of the life of the Lord Jesus, is that one thing was always uppermost in his thinking. It was to do the will of his heavenly Father. It is clear, then, that obedience to the will of God includes within its scope obedience to human authority. God's authority comes to expression in our daily lives by means of people whom he has invested with his authority over us. Why is it, in other words, that children ought to obey their parents? Is it simply because they are bigger? What if a child grows up to become bigger than his parents? Would the tables then be turned, as it were? Would it then be the duty of the parents to obey the child? Again, let us ask, why should we as citizens obey police officers or judges? Well, the answer may seem obvious enough to us, but it certainly is not obvious to some supposedly intelligent people today. One well-known American sociologist wrote an article some years ago for the *Saturday Review*. In this article she quite seriously proposed—as a great idea for the dawning of a new age—that parents should begin obeying their children! This was her basic thesis: the older generation has tried and failed; so the only hope is for the older generation to quit trying to mold the young and instead let the younger generation take the lead. Well, this is the sort of thing that people end up with when they leave the true God and his commandments out of their thinking.

It is certainly true that the older generation has failed. But so did the one before that, and the one before that, and so on right back to Adam. Yet matters would be much worse than they are without those who—to some extent, at least—have kept this commandment. And who are the ones who—to some extent, at least—have kept this commandment? The answer is clear: they are God's covenant people. And look at the result. God promised Abraham that he would be a God to him and his children after him through all generations. The promise attached to this commandment was that their days would be long in the land which the Lord would give to them. The meaning is clear. If there would be faithful observance of the fifth commandment, there would also be covenant blessings. These blessings would include an increase in the average length of life among such people and a long tenure on the portion of the earth that God gave them.

If anything needs urgent attention in the church today, it is the quality of covenant living in the context of the family. Fathers must lead. Parents (the earliest and by far the most influential teachers of their own children) must diligently communicate their deepest convictions to their children. There must be clear lines of authority and discipline in the home. And consistency is of the utmost importance. When children do what is right, they must be consistently praised. And when they do wrong, they must be consistently corrected—sometimes with corporal punishment. Above all other principles, parents must insist on obedience from their children.

Yet, sad to say, it is too often true that this point is neglected even by Christian parents. For instance, a little child accidentally knocks over an expensive lamp. He gets clobbered. Why? Because Mom wanted that lamp, that's why! But then, when the pastor comes to visit, the same Mom says to her little son, "Johnny, it's time to pick up your toys." No response. A little later she says again, "Johnny, I told you to pick up your toys." Still there is no response. Then Mom laughs and says—fully expecting the pastor to laugh too—"I just can't seem to get him to mind me." But, then, she does nothing further. Yet it is in this instance, rather than the other, that the rod ought to be used, because this is a serious infraction. Whenever a child fails to obey the spoken word of father or mother, it is a serious matter for that reason alone. It has very little to do with the magnitude of the particular instruction that has just been given. The importance lies in the fact that God requires children to obey their parents. If a child doesn't learn that from his parents, how—and where—is he going to learn obedience?

Here, then, is the place to begin. Young fathers and mothers, if you want to build up the church, start at home. Start by teaching your children to understand the one thing the Bible says to them directly. Yes, that is right. There is one and only one message that God speaks directly to children when they are little: "Children, obey your parents." If we allow our children to grow up without understanding that, then we fail completely as parents. But if we teach them this one thing consistently, even when it isn't easy, we build a solid foundation in them for life in the two kingdoms. They will know how to respect the civil authorities (Rom. 13:1–5) and how to obey the ruling elders (Heb. 13:17). And most important of all, they will be blessed by God—for it is only a life regulated by God-given authority that God blesses.

QUESTIONS ON THE LESSON

1. Why do parents have authority over their children?
2. What does the example of Jesus prove with respect to this commandment?

3. What is the primary duty of parents to their own children?
4. Give an example of the way in which parents too often ignore this commandment.
5. What does God say directly to children in the Scriptures?

QUESTIONS FOR STUDY AND DISCUSSION

1. Is the fifth commandment one that parents have to keep as well? Explain.
2. Ought we always to obey the civil rulers? What if they command us to train our children in atheistic philosophy, as is done in China?
3. Why do many teenagers today refuse to obey their parents?

Lord's Day 40

SCRIPTURE READINGS: *Genesis 9:5–7;*
Matthew 5:21–26, 43–48; Romans 13:1–7

105. Q. What does God require in the sixth commandment?

A. That I, neither in thought, nor in word or gesture, much less in deed, dishonor, hate, wound, or kill my neighbor, whether by myself or by another, but lay aside all desire of revenge; moreover, that I harm not myself nor wilfully expose myself to any danger. Therefore, also, the magistrate is armed with the sword to prevent murder.

106. Q. But this commandment seems to speak only of murder?

A. In forbidding murder, God teaches us that He abhors the root of murder, as envy, hatred, anger, and desire of revenge; and that He accounts all these as murder.

107. Q. But is it enough that we do not kill our neighbor in any such way?

A. No; for when God forbids envy, hatred, and anger, He commands us to love our neighbor as ourselves: to show patience, peace, meekness, mercy, and all kindness towards him, prevent his hurt as much as in us lies, and do good even to our enemies.

When our Lord was on earth, the "church" was in a bad way. One of the primary reasons for this was that the scribes and Pharisees had made the law of God of no effect by means of their tradition (see Mark 7). They did not *say*, "We reject the fifth commandment." They simply *in-*

terpreted it in such a way as to greatly reduce its demands. But our Lord tells us (in Matt. 5:7–48) that the Ten Commandments demand nothing less than perfection (v. 48). Thus, if we even desire to have sex with another man's wife, we break the seventh commandment just as truly (though not as flagrantly) as if we had committed the physical act of adultery. And this same principle applies to the sixth commandment. We sometimes say, "If looks could kill, then he would be dead." This expresses a deep insight. There are such things as murderous thoughts, and we are all prone to this evil—just as we are also prone to let our thoughts come out in destructive words or gestures.

There was a certain Jew who came very close to death in a German concentration camp during World War II. But the Allied forces came just in time to save his life. However, the camp commandant managed to escape. For years he was on the wanted list of war criminals, and there were Jews who made it their full-time business to track these criminals down. Well, they finally found this man. Imagine the feelings of this Jew when—after more than forty years—he at last faced the man who had murdered so many of his friends and relatives and had almost killed him! Suddenly the Jew burst into tears. When he at last composed himself, someone asked him why he had done that. He gave a surprising answer. It was not because of the evil that he saw in that captured German. No, he said, it was because of what he saw in himself. For he realized, from the depth of hatred in his own heart, how much he had become like this commandant. Let us hope he went beyond this and learned to understand what the Bible means when it says that vengeance belongs to God and not to us (Heb. 10:30).

The only way that we can cease to be murderers is to learn what it means to be truly forgiven. The Bible says that we were originally the objects of God's wrath, just like other people (Eph. 2:3). Yet God did not destroy us. On the contrary, he sent Jesus to die for us. Therefore, our whole existence now rests on the premise of divine forgiveness— even though we are, by nature, hell-deserving sinners. When we comprehend this, it humbles us so much that we begin to think in an entirely different way about others. We understand why Stephen, for example, did not hate those who stoned him to death but prayed for their salvation (Acts 7:59–60). The opposite of murder, in other words, is not indifference to others. It is not a "live and let live" attitude. No, the opposite of murder is love. We are to love others who were made in the image of God even if they are our enemies. We are to recognize that just as God has had mercy on us in bringing us to conversion, so he can do the same for others. There was a time when Saul of Tarsus perpetrated great evil against the church. He was, at that time, what we could well call an accessory to murder (Acts 22:19–20). But after God brought him to conversion, he became one of God's greatest servants and one of the greatest missionaries that the church ever had.

Thus far we have considered the sixth commandment as it applies to the individual Christian. But we also need to understand that it applies to our civil rulers (such as the president of the United States or the prime minister of England). The Scripture says that God has armed civil rulers with the power of the sword (Rom. 13:1–7) in order to put fear into the hearts of those who do evil.

So, when a foreign nation threatens to invade our nation, or begins to kill our citizens by acts of terrorism, it is the duty of those who have been given this power of the sword to use it to prevent these acts of murder. When this is done there will, of course, be the death of human beings. Just as a policeman may have to kill a criminal in the performance of his duties, so a soldier in our armed forces may have to kill certain people from an aggressor nation in the performance of his duties. But it is important to add this: they should not be motivated by personal hatred or vengeance when they do it. No, there should be genuine sorrow over the loss of life. And there should never be cruel treatment of prisoners. The fact that our people are mistreated by the aggressor nation does not in the least justify our mistreatment of their people whom we take captive.

There should be no doubt about one thing: it is entirely legitimate for the chief civil authority of our nation to act against an aggressor. If he does not do this, if he permits state-sponsored terrorism to go unchallenged, he has not exercised the power given to him by God to protect the citizens of his nation. The Heidelberg Catechism is thoroughly biblical in saying that "the magistrate is armed with the sword to prevent murder."

It should be clear to anyone that the sixth commandment can be understood correctly only in the light of the rest of the Bible. This is true, of course, of all of the Ten Commandments. It is for this reason that we agree on one basic thing with John Calvin. In his great commentary on the law, Calvin treated all of the so-called "case laws" given by Moses. He classified every one of these laws, in fact, under the heading of one or another of the Ten Commandments. He saw, in every one of these case laws, principles of universal validity.

The Ten Commandments state the broad principles of the will of God for man. But how do we apply these broad principles in the variety of situations that we encounter in life? Well, the various case laws were given to answer this question. As we study them, we come to a clear understanding of the way in which we are to apply the Ten Commandments. A study of these case laws also tends to keep us from being deceived by those who would make a false use of a particular commandment. Take, for instance, those who oppose capital punishment. You will often hear them quoting the very words of the commandment: "You shall not kill." And then they say, "The execution of a murderer is just another act of murder." But the God who gave us the general principle (the sixth commandment) also gave us particular examples of its correct application (in the case laws). Therefore, when we see how God himself applies the general principle, we will not be deceived by such misrepresentations.

Love is the ultimate antidote to murder. And the Scripture says that there is only one way that we can obtain this as our own possession.

> This is love, not that we loved God, but that He loved us and sent His Son to be the propitiation for our sins. Beloved, if God so loved us, we also ought to love one another. . . . Beloved, let us love one another, for love is of God; and everyone who loves is born of God and knows God. He who does not love does not know God, for God is love. (1 John 4:10–11, 7–8)

Only as we come to understand what we are by nature (in our lost condition)—and what Jesus did to redeem us—will we begin to look at the other man (who is also worthy of eternal death) with a desire for his salvation. This ought to be in the civil magistrate's heart, even if he has to order the execution of a man in the line of his God-given duty.

QUESTIONS ON THE LESSON

1. How did the scribes and Pharisees make the law of God of no effect?
2. In contrast to this, what did our Lord say the commandments require?
3. Why is it so important to study the case laws of the Old Testament?
4. Does this commandment forbid all killing? If not, give some examples of lawful killing.

QUESTIONS FOR STUDY AND DISCUSSION

1. Since hatred is in fact murder, according to the teaching of our Lord, should the civil rulers punish anyone who hates another person, just as they punish a murderer?
2. Every commandment has a positive as well as a negative side. Give some examples of what this commandment means on the positive side.
3. Is abortion a violation of this commandment? Explain.
4. The Old Testament clearly teaches that convicted murderers should be put to death. Should this sentence still be enforced? Why? And what means of execution should be used?

LORD'S DAY 41

SCRIPTURE READINGS: *Romans 1:24–32;*
1 Corinthians 6:9–7:7; Philippians 4:8

108. Q. What does the seventh commandment teach us?
   A. That all unchastity is accursed of God; and that we must,
      therefore, detest it from the heart, and live a chaste and
      continent life both within and outside of holy wedlock.

**109. Q. Does God in this commandment forbid nothing more
      than adultery and such like gross sins?**
   A. Since our body and soul are both temples of the Holy
      Spirit, it is His will that we keep both pure and holy;
      wherefore He forbids all unchaste actions, gestures, words,
      thoughts, desires, and whatever may entice one thereto.

When the Heidelberg Catechism was written, it was not necessary to
speak of some things that we must openly discuss today. There was no
need, for example, to make explicit mention of homosexual behavior.
Today there is. There has been so much degeneration in public moral-
ity that many in our society now regard homosexual practice as an acceptable way of life. Even more tragic is the fact that some supposedly
Christian churches have now taken a permissive attitude toward such
abominations. We say "abominations" advisedly, because this is the way
God himself speaks in Scripture about the sin of homosexual behavior.

   The reader should not misunderstand. We do not suggest that this
is the "unpardonable sin." Not at all. As a matter of fact, one of our
reasons for mentioning this sin is that it is not the unpardonable sin,
just as it is also not an incurable condition. We know this from the

Bible. The apostle Paul clearly says in 1 Corinthians 6:9–11 that some of the members of the church at Corinth had once been homosexuals and that they had been washed, justified, and sanctified. What a glorious thing it is that the gospel of the Lord Jesus Christ is *"the power of God to salvation for everyone who believes"* (Rom. 1:16), including the homosexual pervert. No, neither a homosexual desire nor a homosexual act is unpardonable. But homosexuality certainly can lead to eternal damnation. As a matter of fact, it will—unless there is repentance. That is why it is such a terrible thing when a "church" fails to call homosexuals to repentance and instead condones this sin, thus encouraging people to avoid repentance.

And how is this evil thing being done by some "churches" today? Well, it is done by claiming that some people are just born that way (that is, with an innate homosexual disposition), and that they therefore bear a minimal responsibility for their condition. Now whatever else may be said for this view, one thing is certain—it is not revealed in the Scriptures. To the contrary, the Bible clearly says that we are all depraved by nature. What this means is that the effects of the fall of man—the corruption of our nature—is something that pervades our entire nature and is present in all of us. This means that all of us are, by nature, potential homosexuals (just as we are potential thieves, murderers, adulterers, etc.). If we do not actually become such, it is not because we are inherently better than others. No, it is only because God in his mercy has preserved us from the full outworking of our own corrupt nature.

It is exactly the same with adultery as it is with homosexual sin. It is not just some of us who have the innate capacity—or tendency— to lust after another person's wife or husband. No, the truth is that we all have the root of this sin in our nature. That is why Jesus did not say, "Well, it's too bad, but some of you people are just made that way, and you can't help it when you lust after another man's wife." He never treated any person as if he had a minimal responsibility for his sin. No, the Lord Jesus simply condemned it.

And right here we would ask a pointed question. By what right is the homosexual sinner treated as something special? What about a person who molests little children? Can we also say that this is a "sickness" that afflicts some members of the human race who just "cannot help it"? No, of course not. The Bible says this is sin. It is a sin that all of us by nature would be quite capable of, if it were not for God's grace. (There are unbelievers who are restrained by God, in various ways, from being homosexual. This is sometimes called "common grace," meaning the restraining influences that God brings to bear on men outside the covenant. The regenerate, of course, are restrained from "within" by God's Spirit when he makes them new creatures in Christ.)

The Bible says that each of us is responsible for his own sexual behavior. And the church should be warning us—fearlessly and uncompromisingly—that sin is sin, and that we are fully responsible for the sins that we commit. Then the church should go on to show us how the saving power of Jesus is great enough to redeem every one of us, even the most notorious sinner. Those who do not believe this anymore should be honest enough to admit it. If they are pastors, elders, or deacons, they should resign their office in the church and honestly admit—to the people—that they no longer believe that "the gospel of Christ is the power of God for salvation." The Heidelberg Catechism makes absolutely no concession to sin. It demands—because Scripture demands—our entire perfection. It condemns all unchastity, whether within or outside of marriage. And it not only condemns the sinful act, but anything and everything that may incite it.

When the Catechism was written, there was no such thing as television. Yet observe how clearly our historic instructor speaks (by means of principle) about its insidious influence. Can anyone watch the majority of programs today, in which unchastity is constantly minimized and even made to seem innocent and attractive, without a seriously corrupting effect? I once knew a husband and wife who were born and raised in Holland. When they were young, they moved to a new country. Many years later they went back "home" for a visit. The thing that shocked them was this: their own parents, who had once seemed so godly to them, were watching vile things on television without a murmur of complaint. But how did it happen? It did not happen all at once. No, it happened little by little. It is said that you can boil a frog to death if you just increase the temperature very slowly. The change in the temperature is so gradual that the frog does not realize what is happening to it. So it can be, too, with the effects of television. We are not saying that television is evil in itself. But we are warning of the danger and suggesting that all of us need to be far more diligent in regulating it. There are some good things on television today, but there are also many more that are evil. And God knows how prone we all are to respond positively to that which is evil. That is why he forbids "all unchaste actions, gestures, words, thoughts, desires, and whatever may entice one thereto."

The antidote to adultery is, or should be—for most of us—a good marriage. This means a marriage in which there is the right kind of sexual fulfillment. Sex is not evil. How could it be, when God himself designed it? And because it is one of the good gifts of God, it must not be neglected. What do we mean by this statement? Well, we mean this: in every other aspect of life we have to apply some real effort in order to achieve something. This is true for a farmer in his work, or an amateur musician in his hobby, or a Saturday golfer in his sport. We invest time and effort in these things, in order to do them well and to keep them interesting and exciting. Well, a good sexual relationship requires some of the same. To put it bluntly: it is your duty to be creative in serving the sexual needs of your husband or wife. In my pastoral ministry, I have seen cases of adultery where the lack of this has definitely been a contributing factor. The husband or wife would not have begun to be attracted to someone else so readily if there had not been a prior failure in the fulfillment of sexual needs at home. This does not excuse adultery, but it does help to explain it. There is no legitimate place for prudery in Christian marriage. A Christian husband or wife should make sex such an exciting thing for his or her spouse that the adulterous relationship will not be appealing. If you are not convinced of this yet, then you need to study the Song of Solomon. God gave us this inspired book about sex for one simple reason. He wanted to show us how much better this gift can be when it is fully expressed in marriage than it can ever be in any illicit affair.

What the world needs today is a demonstration of the truth of the Bible. And where is that witness needed more than in the realm of sex and marriage? There is perhaps no Christian witness that we can give today that will have more impact and meaning than to display before the eyes of the watching world the beauty of happy marriages and godly Christian families. The Catechism calls us to this lofty goal in its treatment of the seventh commandment.

QUESTIONS ON THE LESSON

1. Why does the Catechism make no direct mention of homosexual sin?
2. Cite biblical proof that all homosexual acts are sinful—but are also forgivable.
3. State the two main errors taught in some churches today with respect to homosexual behavior.

4. Why is it a sin to indulge in entertainment (TV, for instance) that minimizes and even promotes sexual sin?
5. What is the biblical antidote to adultery (see 1 Cor. 7:1–2)?

QUESTIONS FOR STUDY AND DISCUSSION

1. What aspects of our culture other than TV incite people to unchastity?
2. In light of this commandment, how would you evaluate the current practices of dating and of having roommates of the opposite sex?
3. What is the positive side of this commandment? What things are required by this commandment?

Lord's Day 42

SCRIPTURE READINGS: *Deuteronomy 25:13–16;*
Ephesians 4:28; 2 Thessalonians 3:6–15

110. Q. What does God forbid in the eighth commandment?

A. God forbids not only such theft and robbery as are punished by the magistrate, but He also brands as theft all
wicked tricks and devices whereby we aim to appropriate
our neighbor's goods, whether by force or with show of
right, as unjust weights, ells, measures, and wares, false
coins, usury, or any other means forbidden by God; likewise all covetousness and all abuse and waste of His gifts.

111. Q. But what does God require of you in this commandment?

A. That I further my neighbor's profit wherever I can or
may, deal with him as I would have others deal with me,
and labor faithfully that I may be able to relieve the
needy.

It is interesting to note some of the Old Testament proof texts for this
section of the Catechism. One of them is Deuteronomy 25:13–16, which
reads:

> *You shall not have in your bag differing weights, a heavy and a light.*
> *You shall not have in your house differing measures, a large and a*
> *small. You shall have a perfect and just weight, a perfect and just mea-*
> *sure, that your days may be lengthened in the land which the LORD*
> *your God is giving you. For all who do such things, and all who be-*
> *have unrighteously, are an abomination to the LORD your God.*

The commandment here is expressed in terms of everyday life as it was in the time of Moses. In those days people carried weights in a bag so they could determine the corresponding weight of the things they bought and sold. Today we do not carry weights in a bag for this purpose. But the principle is quite clearly valid, always and everywhere. The principle is that we must have only one standard, and it must be the correct one. We are not free to use one standard with someone we like and another standard with someone we do not like. We are not free to cheat anyone by the use of deceptive standards of measure. The reason is quite simple: such acts are nothing more than stealing.

Stealing can be defined as the act of taking something that we have no right to take. In contrast to this, there are three ways that we can obtain things without stealing. First, we can obtain things by way of inheritance. If a wealthy man dies, leaving his wealth to his children, then they have a right to take what once belonged to their father. Second, we can obtain things by receiving a gift. If a man with great wealth decides to give a million dollars to one of his faithful servants, that servant has a perfect right to take it. Third, we can obtain things legitimately in wages paid for our labor. If I perform a certain amount of work for an employer, and he pays me an agreed amount of money at the end of the week, then that is not stealing. Again, it is not stealing if I go out as a pioneer to hack a clearing out of an uninhabited jungle. If I turn this into productive land, I have a right to the things produced from it. But apart from these three ways of obtaining wealth, there is no other legitimate way to get money. Yet such is the sinful nature of man that he tries to invent a thousand ways to steal from his fellows.

Take gambling, for instance. Now what is gambling if it is not a form of stealing? True, in many forms of gambling today this fact is somewhat hidden. Ten thousand people buy "a chance." Each of them has the hope, however, that he will be the one who gets something for practically nothing. Each buyer of a ticket hopes that for $1.00 (let us say) he will be the "lucky winner" who gets the new car. Sometimes the evil is even further hidden by the fact that some of the money is set aside for a charitable cause. Yet in actual fact this side effect is beside the point. The point is that everyone who buys a ticket *desires* to get something for practically nothing. And that is exactly contrary to this commandment. Furthermore, each gambler hopes that everyone else will get nothing in exchange for their dollars so that he can get them for himself. And that is closely akin to stealing. And then, to compound the evil, there is the fact that the people who organize these raffles are usually the real "winners." By that we mean that they rake in plenty of money for themselves in exchange for practically nothing. So the whole thing—disguised or not—is in fact against this commandment. These are "all wicked tricks and devices whereby we aim to appropriate our neighbor's goods." And it is no answer to this to say, "Yes, but they know they have a very small chance of winning, so they are really willing to part with their money." The Bible doesn't say it is permissible to cheat and swindle our neighbor so long as he knows we are likely to do it.

It is bad enough when individuals do this to each other. It is much worse when this is institutionalized, as it is today, by various state lotteries. The argument often used for these is that they provide needed income for the state. This too is a fraudulent claim, because it promotes a sinful greed in the hearts of the people. It encourages them to want to get rich quick, without any hard work or frugality. It is true, of course, that we read now and then about some factory worker who becomes a millionaire. What we do not read is the rest of the story—the story of thousands of little children who go without proper food because Dad or Mom has taken grocery money to place a bet on the horses. It will never be right for one man to get rich at the expense of these suffering children. God requires us to do what we can for the good of our neighbors, and that means treating them as we would like them to treat us—and that includes these little children.

There was a lot of stealing going on in society when the New Testament Scriptures were written. But God did not make any concession to this evil. To people converted out of that society this is what he said: *"Let him who stole steal no longer, but rather let him labor, working with his hands what is good, that he may have something to give him who has need"* (Eph. 4:28). And that is not all. He also said: *"If anyone will not work, neither shall he eat"* (2 Thess. 3:10). In our culture today, these principles are widely disregarded. People who are not willing to work are supported by tax money. This means that the state is taking money from people who do work in order to give it to people who do not want to work. What is this if it is not a form of stealing? And is it not the task of a faithful church today to testify against this prevalent evil? We believe it is. One of the ways the church can do this is by faithfully disciplining its members, so that no one who belongs to the church is allowed to practice this evil.

QUESTIONS ON THE LESSON

1. What does the "case law" found in Deuteronomy 25:13–16 show us?
2. What are the three legitimate ways in which our own wealth may be increased?
3. How is the sin of stealing disguised in various forms of gambling?
4. Why are state lotteries wrong?
5. What evils result from state-sponsored forms of gambling?

QUESTIONS FOR STUDY AND DISCUSSION

1. Can you think of other forms of state-sponsored stealing that are prevalent today?
2. When the state taxes its citizens, is that stealing? What about inheritance taxes?
3. Is it ever right to receive welfare from the government? From whom does this money come?
4. How should a society provide for its truly poor?

LORD'S DAY 43

SCRIPTURE READINGS: *Matthew 5:33–37;*
1 Samuel 16; Ephesians 4:15, 25

112. Q. What is required in the ninth commandment?

A. That I bear false witness against no man; wrest no one's
words; be no backbiter or slanderer; do not judge, or join
in condemning, any man rashly or unheard; but that I
avoid all sorts of lies and deceit as the proper works of the
devil, unless I would bring down upon myself the heavy
wrath of God; likewise, that in judicial and all other deal-
ings I love the truth, speak it uprightly, and confess it; and
that, as much as I am able, I defend and promote the honor
and reputation of my neighbor.

In giving us the Ten Commandments, God chose the concrete rather
than the abstract. That is, one specific example is used to illustrate a
general principle. In the ninth commandment, the concrete example is
the sin of giving false testimony in a court of law. This is a particularly
heinous sin because those who give testimony are at least implicitly under oath and thus under solemn obligation to God to tell the truth, the
whole truth, and nothing but the truth. Yet such is the tendency of man
to lie, even under such solemn circumstances, that the law required at
least two or three witnesses, so that the testimony of one witness might
be confirmed by another (Deut. 17:6).

The teaching of Jesus, however, clearly shows that there is implicit
in this commandment the duty to tell the truth at all times and in every
situation (Matt. 5:33–37). Some have incorrectly concluded from his
teaching that it is wrong to give sworn testimony. But Jesus did not say

that anything more than a simple yes or no answer is evil. What he said was that anything more than this *comes from* (the prevalence of) evil. In other words, because lying is so rampant, it is necessary at times to answer under oath. The Christian, however, should strive more and more to speak at all times in the same careful and truthful manner that he would while under oath.

Here, once again, the Heidelberg Catechism displays a brilliant insight. If "all sorts of lies and deceit" are the "works of the devil," it follows that Christians should renounce them once and for all. As the apostle Paul put it, *"We have renounced the hidden things of shame, not walking in craftiness nor handling the word of God deceitfully"* (2 Cor. 4:2). But, someone may ask, What if your very life is at stake? Is it really a sin to lie in that situation? There are some, today, who claim to be biblical and yet allow, or even advocate, lying in such circumstances. They reason that it is sometimes necessary to lie because that is the only thing that can save a person from death. But is this really true? Is it true, for instance, that we can ever know in advance what will—or will not—happen to us if we are faithful to God? And again, do we really know that God will not work providentially to save us if we trust in him? We believe the following true story is worth thinking about.

Kim Duk-Soo became an administrator of a Presbyterian hospital in Taegu, Korea. He was the son of a Presbyterian pastor who had served the same church for 42 years. He will never forget November 20, 1950, the day the Communist troops found him hiding with his father in a root cellar. His father had always told him that he should never lie, not even to try to save his own life. He remembered this when he and his father were led off to a makeshift prison, knowing that they were to be executed the next morning. But later that evening, a North Korean captain approached Kim and asked: "Are you a Christian?" For a fleeting moment, life for a lie seemed the only sensible option. But then he remembered the words of his father. "Yes," he said, "I am a Christian." To his surprise, the captain then drew closer and whispered, "I am a Christian, too. I used to be a Sunday school teacher before the war. You must escape tonight, and I will help you." So he escaped, and it was not because he lied in a time of trial, but because he remembered the words of his father—words that said the very same thing that we find in this catechism question.

It is important to note, however, that God does not require us to reveal everything we know to be true to his and our enemies. God himself clearly sanctioned a partial concealment of truth (1 Sam. 16) when there was reason to believe that a full revelation of it would provoke evil. God sent Samuel to anoint David as King of Israel. But, in order to conceal this from King Saul, the Lord instructed Samuel also to take a sacrifice along with him and to say, "*I have come to sacrifice to the LORD*" (v. 5). This was not a lie because he really did come there to sacrifice, as God had commanded. But Samuel did not reveal all that was true. He was directed by God to conceal some of the truth. From this we learn that what we say must be the truth, but that we are not required to tell everything that is true.

Lying is very common in our culture today, so common in fact that in many forms it is not even recognized for what it is. Take flattery, for example. Many people who are prominent today in the political realm, or the mass media, flatter one another with praise and adulation. We are reminded daily of the complaint of the psalmist: "*Help, LORD, for the godly man ceases! For the faithful disappear from among the sons of men. They speak idly everyone with his neighbor; With flattering lips and a double heart they speak. May the LORD cut off all flattering lips*" (Ps. 12:1–3). Or, again, think of gossip. Because of our inherent sinfulness, we have a tendency to take delight in an evil report. As the proverb says, "*The words of a gossip are like choice morsels*" (Prov. 18:8, NIV). Yet the Bible says that we should not even listen to an accusation against one of the elders of the church unless there are two or three witnesses (1 Tim. 5:19). In the book of Titus, the apostle Paul quotes with agreement a characterization of the people of Crete written by one of their own people. He said, "*Cretans are always liars*" (1:12). From this we see how various forms of lying can become so rampant in a society that they are accepted as normal by almost everyone. But what does Paul instruct Titus to do as he ministers to those people? Does he tell him to ignore this, since it was not looked upon as a serious evil by the Cretans? No, what he says is this: "*This testimony is true. Therefore rebuke them sharply*" (v. 13).

QUESTIONS ON THE LESSON

1. Why does each commandment refer to a specific sin, rather than to an abstract, general principle?
2. What did Jesus mean when he said: "*Let your 'Yes' be 'Yes,' and your 'No,' 'No.' For whatever is more than these is from the evil one*" (Matt. 5:37)?

3. What false assumption is sometimes made by those who argue that lying is at times justified?
4. What proof can you give to show that it is not always a sin to reveal only part of the truth while at the same time concealing part of it?
5. What does Paul's remark in Titus 1:12–13 teach us?
6. Can the same thing be said of people in our society today?

QUESTIONS FOR STUDY AND DISCUSSION

1. How would you reconcile the lie that Rahab told in Joshua 2:4–5 and the Lord's approval of her in Hebrews 11:31 and James 2:25 with God's condemnation of lying?
2. Is lying to and deceiving the enemy proper in war? Can a Christian be a good soldier or military strategist?
3. List several different situations in which you are tempted to lie. How do you deal with those situations?

LORD'S DAY 44

SCRIPTURE READINGS: *Colossians 2:20–3:17; 1 John 5:1–4*

113. Q. What does the tenth commandment require of us?

A. That not even the slightest inclination or thought contrary to any of God's commandments shall ever rise in our heart; but that at all times we shall hate all sin with our whole heart and delight in all righteousness.

114. Q. But can those who are converted to God keep these commandments perfectly?

A. No; but even the holiest men, while in this life, have only a small beginning of this obedience; yet so that with earnest purpose they begin to live, not only according to some but according to all the commandments of God.

115. Q. Why, then, will God have the ten commandments preached so strictly, since in this life no one can keep them?

A. First, that all our life long we may learn more and more to know our sinful nature, and so become the more earnest in seeking remission of sins and righteousness in Christ; second, that we may constantly endeavor, and pray to God for the grace of the Holy Spirit, to be renewed more and more after the image of God, till after this life we arrive at the goal of perfection.

The Pharisees were masters of deceit. They tried to appear as zealous upholders of the law, while in actual fact they made the law of no effect through their traditions (Mark 7:1–13). Jesus compared them to cups washed on the outside but filthy on the inside—and to graves whitewashed on the outside but full of dead men's bones within (Matt. 23:25–28). Their primary error was that they were only concerned with external, visible actions. As long as a person did a number of prescribed things, outwardly, and avoided certain proscribed things, he was considered blameless. We find the same mentality in some evangelical churches. I once served in a church that reduced godliness to abstaining from a short list of things forbidden—chiefly alcoholic beverages. As long as one totally abstained from alcohol, one would be considered a godly person. Yet in actual fact, it was often not so.

The apostle Paul grew up in this type of religious environment. He observed whatever was prescribed and avoided whatever was proscribed by the Pharisees' tradition. But, as he himself later testified, there was one commandment that he just couldn't handle (Rom. 7:7). It was the tenth commandment. The reason for this is quite simple: this commandment does not deal with external action, but with internal desire. And the Pharisees had never been able to invent a way to make this law void by means of their tradition. We could say, then, that the tenth commandment is unique. It differs from the other nine in that it deals entirely with thought and desire. And because of this, it also qualifies all of the other commandments. The eighth commandment, in other words, already tells me that I must not steal my neighbor's ox or donkey. But this commandment shows me that I must not even desire to do this! Again, the seventh commandment already tells me that I must not commit adultery with my neighbor's wife. But this commandment shows me that I sin if I even desire to do this.

We properly understand the tenth commandment only when we realize that Jesus was right when he said that it is our duty to be perfect, even as our Father in heaven is perfect (Matt. 5:48).

It is also worthy of note that the apostle Paul says that covetousness (breaking the tenth commandment) is idolatry (breaking the first commandment) (Col. 3:5). This is true because the law is a unity. We are reminded, here, of the vandal who attacked Rembrandt's famous painting *The Night Watch* in an Amsterdam museum. He slashed only part of that incomparable painting. But in so doing he damaged the whole painting. So it is with God's law. If I kept the first commandment perfectly, I would never even begin to violate the others. Whenever we sin, we begin to depart from God. And so, as the apostle says (in Col. 3:5), the moment we even desire what God has forbidden, we are really forsaking the true God in order to serve an idol (a false god). And right here is the hallmark of the genuine Christian. He is a new creature. He has been born again from above. He has been brought into union with Jesus. And so, already in this life, he begins to delight in the law of God and wants to keep his commandments. Take the apostle Paul, for example. After his conversion, he says, he came to delight in the law of God (Rom. 7:22). Likewise, the apostle John says that God's commandments are not an unpleasant burden to the genuine Christian (1 John 5:3). It is not the case that Christians can claim perfection. To the contrary, even the holiest believers—as the Catechism says—have only a small beginning of that obedience which the law requires. But they *do* have a beginning. And they also have a desire to press on to perfection.

QUESTIONS ON THE LESSON

1. How does the tenth commandment differ from the other nine?
2. Give an example of emphasizing external regulations while neglecting the desires of the heart.
3. Why does Paul call covetousness idolatry?
4. Since no one can keep the Ten Commandments perfectly, what is different about the true believer?
5. Are the first nine commandments concerned about the intentions of the heart?

QUESTIONS FOR STUDY AND DISCUSSION

1. Do God's people keep his commandments? Explain.
2. Can God's people keep his commandments? Explain.
3. For what reasons should the Ten Commandments be preached today?
4. Should they be preached to believers or only to unbelievers?

LORD'S DAY 45

SCRIPTURE READINGS: *Psalm 16;*
Matthew 6:1–15; Romans 8:26–30

116. Q. Why is prayer necessary for Christians?
   A. Because it is the chief part of the thankfulness which God
   requires of us, and because God will give His grace and
   Holy Spirit to those only who with hearty sighing unceas-
   ingly beg them of Him and thank Him for them.

**117. Q. What belongs to such prayer as God is pleased with and
   will hear?**
   A. First, that from the heart we call upon the one true God
   only, who has revealed Himself in His Word, for all He has
   commanded us to ask of Him; second, that we right thoroughly know our need and misery, in order to humble ourselves before the face of His majesty; third, that we be
   firmly assured that, notwithstanding we are unworthy of it,
   He will, for the sake of Christ our Lord, certainly hear our
   prayer, as He has promised us in His Word.

118. Q. What has God commanded us to ask of Him?
   A. All things necessary for soul and body, which Christ our
   Lord has comprised in the prayer He Himself has taught us.

119. Q. What is the Lord's Prayer?
   A. *Our Father who art in heaven,*
   Hallowed be thy name;
   Thy kingdom come;

Thy will be done, as in heaven, so on earth.
Give us this day our daily bread;
And forgive us our debts, as we also have forgiven our debtors;
And bring us not into temptation, but deliver us from the evil
    one.
For thine is the kingdom, and the power, and the glory, for ever.
    Amen.

Prayer is the hallmark of the believer. One who has been born from above can no more live without prayer than the natural man can live without oxygen. For what, after all, is prayer? It is fundamentally the longing aspiration of the regenerate heart for the true God as his portion. It is for this reason that the apostle Paul can speak of prayer in a way that is very different from what many people imagine it to be. They think of prayer as a form of pious words, spoken with a certain tone of voice. But Paul says,

Likewise the Spirit also helps in our weaknesses. For we do not know what we should pray for as we ought, but the Spirit Himself makes intercession for us with groanings which cannot be uttered. Now He who searches the hearts knows what the mind of the Spirit is, because He makes intercession for the saints according to the will of God. (Rom. 8:26–27)

A person who can stand up in public and pour out a torrent of eloquent words is often thought to be mighty in prayer. In actual fact, the man who is too choked up to express more than a groan or a sigh may really be praying in a manner that is more pleasing to God.

The reason for this is clearly explained in the Catechism. In the first place, prayer will never be acceptable to God unless it comes from the heart. The trouble with eloquent speech is that it can become attractive because of its form. It can also generate the praise of men. Vocal prayer does, as a matter of fact, become a means by which some people attract attention to themselves and bolster their own self-esteem. But what matters is not how we impress men, but rather what God thinks of our praying. And God does not think much of it unless it takes account of the two great things that constitute the very outline of the first two parts of the Catechism. In the second place, we need to realize our own complete unworthiness, in order to pray an acceptable prayer to God, as the first part of the Catechism teaches. If we only realized our true condition and position as fallen men before God, we would certainly see ourselves as nothing in comparison with God's majestic being. Like the publican in the parable of Jesus, we would cast our eyes down and smite our own breasts, saying, *"God be merciful to me a sinner!"* (Luke 18:13). In the third place, we must also realize that we have no right to the things for which we are pleading. The second part of the Catechism teaches that all we receive from God is by grace (unmerited favor). Therefore, genuine prayer must always be a humble asking for unmerited favors, and the only basis for expecting that God will answer us graciously is his own covenant promise.

What is prayer? It is just true religion coming to expression as a constant necessity in the believer. And this is true because—for the real child of God—all of life is religion. This is just as true when it comes to our daily bread as it is when it comes to Satan's temptations. It is just as true when we are praying for the little things in our daily lives as it is when we are praying for things that are momentous. And if we understand what we are by nature (or were, before we were made alive unto Jesus), we will see that there is no such thing as acceptable prayer without the mediation of Jesus. It is only because of what Christ has done for us in the past, and because of what he is now doing, that we can come to the exalted and holy God of the Bible with the hope that he will listen!

Of course, the natural man will try to pray when he faces a crisis. He knows that God is there, and in time of great need he may cry out to him for mercy. But only the Christian is able to pray not only in humility but also with confident expectation. And he can do this because God has told us that he will listen to us if we come in—and through— the Lord Jesus. The prayer of the natural man will therefore stand in marked contrast to the prayer of the believer. And the model prayer that Jesus gave his disciples helps us to see this clearly. After all, what is the basic difference between the natural man and the spiritual man? Well, the answer is quite simple: the natural man is still under the power of sin, while the spiritual man has been delivered. And what is the result when the power of sin and the power of Satan have dominion over man's heart and mind? Well, the answer is that man makes himself the one who is central. The "prayer" of the natural man begins with self. The big "I" will come to the forefront just as it did with the Pharisee in the parable of the Lord Jesus: *"God, I thank You that I am not like other men—extortioners, unjust, adulterers, or even as this tax collector. I fast twice a week; I give tithes of all that I possess"* (Luke 18:11). But how different it is with the spiritual man. In his thinking, God is central and man's concerns are subordinate.

Christianity is God-centered. That is why the Ten Commandments and the Lord's Prayer are similar in structure (emphasizing the centrality of God). True prayer is, quite simply, the true religion in its outworking. It is important to observe, then, that Jesus did not say that we should just repeat this prayer. No, what he said was that we should pray after this manner. This prayer, as a great preacher once said, is like a model house in a real-estate office. It was never meant to be a house to live in, but rather a model to build by. But of this we will have more to say in the next section.

QUESTIONS ON THE LESSON

1. What is prayer?
2. Is it only the Christian who can offer acceptable prayer to God? If so, why?
3. Is it possible for a groan or a sigh to be a prayer? Why?
4. What is the relationship between true prayer and true doctrine?
5. How do the prayers of unregenerate and regenerate persons differ?
6. Did Christ say that we should repeat the Lord's Prayer?

QUESTIONS FOR STUDY AND DISCUSSION

1. What does it mean to pray from the heart?
2. Is it possible to *"pray without ceasing,"* as Paul commands in 1 Thessalonians 5:17?
3. Many churches use formal written prayers in their worship. Discuss the merits and demerits of this practice.

LORD'S DAY 46

SCRIPTURE READINGS: *Luke 11:1–13;*
Ephesians 1:1–6; 1 John 3:1–12

120. **Q. Why has Christ commanded us to address God thus, *Our Father?***
   A. To awaken in us, at the very beginning of our prayer, that childlike reverence and trust toward God which should be the ground of our prayer; namely, that God has become our Father through Christ, and will much less deny us what we ask of Him in true faith than our parents will refuse us earthly things.

121. **Q. Why is there added, *Who art in heaven?***
   A. That we may have no earthly thought of the heavenly majesty of God, and may expect from His almighty power all things necessary for body and soul.

"Without faith it is impossible to please [God]" (Heb. 11:6). It is also impossible, without faith, to pray a prayer that God will accept. This is clearly established by the first phrase in the model prayer that Jesus taught his disciples. Although it is commonly assumed that God is the father of all men, and that all men are brothers, this is not what the Scriptures teach. It is true, of course, that God is the Creator of all men, and that all men are related through Adam. If this is what is meant by speaking of "the fatherhood of God and the brotherhood of men," then there would be no reason to object to it. But the Scriptures do not use these terms to describe man in his present fallen condition. No, the Scriptures teach us that man is by nature a child of wrath (Eph. 2:3).

Jesus said that the unbelieving Jews were not, in the true sense, Abraham's children—as they assumed—but were in fact the children of Satan (John 8:44). This is true of all who are not reconciled to God. And the only way that sinful men can be reconciled to God is through faith in Jesus. It is only when we are "in Christ" that we become new creatures. For all who are repentant and are united with Christ by faith have God as their heavenly Father.

But what does this phrase teach us? It teaches us that all true prayer begins with a relationship to the true God. In order for us to pray, the one living and true God, who is in heaven, must also be a loving Father to us. This, in turn, means that God is infinitely far above us. Yet, at the same time, he is close to us, as a father is close to his children. Both of these things are absolutely essential. If either of them is lacking, we will not be able to pray in an acceptable manner. And here we illustrate for clarity.

A certain Hollywood actress once made a public announcement to the effect that she had found "religion." She then began to talk about God in such a way as to make it quite clear that she had no conception whatever of his exalted majesty! She spoke of him as "a nice, indulgent Daddy." And she said that she would just love to run up to him, jump up in his lap, and put her arms around his neck! What a far cry this is from what John saw in the book of Revelation! When John saw God as he really is, exalted in glory, he was overwhelmed with a sense of awe and fear—not terror, such as an unbeliever has, but awe at the greatness of God. The last thing in the world that John would have done would have been to think or talk about God in the way this actress did. At the same time, however, it is equally wrong to think of God as unreachable. In Roman Catholic piety, it is considered a wise and acceptable thing to pray to the virgin Mary or one of the saints. Why? Because they are human and therefore close enough for us to reach. It is then thought that they, because of their superior holiness, can reach God for us. But, of course, there is just as much error in this as there is in the actress's concept of God. The reason is quite simple: Jesus is both God and man. Both the divine nature and the human nature are there in one person. Because in his human nature he is our brother, and in his divine nature is the only begotten Son of God, he can reach both God and man and bring them together.

Rightly understood, in other words, this first phrase teaches us implicitly "that God has become our Father through Christ." It teaches us both childlike awe and trust.

QUESTIONS ON THE LESSON

1. What has to exist before we can pray a prayer acceptable to God?
2. Is God the father of all men? Explain.
3. What are the three essentials of true prayer that are taught by the first phrase of the Lord's Prayer?
4. Which of these elements was evidently lacking in the Hollywood actress?
5. Which of these elements is missing in Roman Catholic prayers through Mary?
6. In contrast to these, describe the two aspects of a proper attitude in prayer.

QUESTIONS FOR STUDY AND DISCUSSION

1. How is it possible to view God both as the Almighty, before whom we are to come with awe, and as a loving Father to whom we may come with all our burdens and needs?
2. Is it really true that God will give us anything we ask for? Provide Scripture proofs for your answer.

LORD'S DAY 47

SCRIPTURE READINGS: *Psalm 99; 2 Samuel 12:1–15*

122. Q. What is the first petition?

A. *Hallowed by thy name*. That is: grant us, first, rightly to know Thee, and to sanctify, glorify, and praise Thee in all Thy works, in which Thy power, wisdom, goodness, justice, mercy, and truth shine forth; further also, that we may so order and direct our whole life, thoughts, words, and actions, that Thy Name may not be blasphemed but honored and praised on our account.

This first petition presents us with a real problem. God's name already *is* holy, so how can it be hallowed? This is like the problem we sense when we are told to glorify God. God is already absolutely glorious, so how can we glorify him? It is perfectly clear that we cannot increase God's glory or add anything to it in any ultimate sense. What it must mean, therefore, is that we can be of service to God as he manifests his own glory. And so it is with the hallowing of his name. God's name is indeed already holy. But it is not recognized as such in the way that it ought to be in this world. What the believer asks in this petition, then, is that God would receive the honor, reverence, worship, and praise to which he is rightly entitled.

It is important to notice the order of the first three petitions. They are concerned with God's name, his kingdom, and his will. Beginning with the last, we could say that as God's will is done, his kingdom comes. And as his kingdom comes, his name is hallowed. This means that even the coming of the kingdom of God—and the doing of his will by his creatures—is a means to the ultimate end of giving him honor and glory.

It is impossible to think of anything that goes more completely contrary to fallen human nature than this first petition. The natural man could not possibly begin a prayer with this as his foremost thought. But it is found in the heart of God's children. True, they may sometimes forget. They may sometimes put too much of self and not enough of God into their prayer. But if true religion is there in their hearts, this will be the basic foundation: their deepest desire will always be that God's name would be hallowed, that is, regarded and treated as holy.

What this means can perhaps be seen more clearly if we think of a particular situation in life. Let us say that you have an unbelieving relative whom you love very dearly. He has often heard the gospel, but has hardened his heart against it. Your natural desire would be to ask God to save him regardless of his sinful rebellion. But if this petition lives in your heart, taking precedence over everything else, you will not be able to ask God to save him as he is. No, instead you will ask God to bring him to repentance and faith, if that be in accord with his sovereign will. But you will also have to say "Thy will be done" if that person is never converted, knowing that—in such a case—it would mean his eternal damnation.

True prayer is not cheap. It is costly. It means that we put God and the Lord Jesus Christ first. Anyone who lacks this basic desire has not even begun to offer acceptable prayer to God.

QUESTIONS ON THE LESSON

1. Why is this petition a "problem"?
2. What is the basic idea that we are really expressing in this petition?
3. How are the first three petitions related?
4. Why is it wrong to ask God to save an unbelieving relative "as is"?

QUESTIONS FOR STUDY AND DISCUSSION

1. The Catechism refers to God's works and all that shines forth from them. How might we hallow God's name through a study of his creation? How will such study affect our prayers?
2. The Catechism also refers to causing God's name to be blasphemed. How did David cause that name to be blasphemed? In what ways might we do this?

LORD'S DAY 48

SCRIPTURE READINGS: *Psalm 110; 1 Corinthians 15:20–28*

123. Q. What is the second petition?

A. *Thy kingdom come.* That is: so rule us by Thy Word and
Spirit that we may submit ourselves more and more to
Thee; preserve and increase Thy Church; destroy the
works of the devil, every power that exalts itself against
Thee, and all wicked counsels conceived against Thy holy
Word, until the perfection of Thy kingdom arrive wherein
Thou shalt be all in all.

Are you a discerning reader? If you are, you probably noticed how different the teaching of this section of the Heidelberg Catechism is from
what is commonly taught in many churches today. What is often taught
today is that the kingdom of God will come, to be sure, but only after
the return of Christ. In the meantime, it is said, we must look for the
coming of the Antichrist. When the Antichrist comes, the church will
be so hard-pressed that it will barely survive. Only the sudden appearance of Christ in glory will stave off the seemingly inevitable defeat.
Then, at last, will his kingdom come. This view of eschatology (meaning "the doctrine of last things") has now become so common that many
people accept it almost without thinking. Yet this view was not shared
by the great Reformers. No, the Reformers saw the kingdom of God as
a present reality. They also believed that it would "come" more and more
in history as the church went forward in its task of carrying the gospel
to the whole world. What is involved in this task was clearly stated by
our Lord Jesus Christ when he gave his church the Great Commission.
He said, "*All authority has been given to Me in heaven and on earth. Go*

therefore and make disciples of all the nations, baptizing them in the name of the Father and of the Son and of the Holy Spirit, teaching them to observe all things that I have commanded you; and lo, I am with you always, even to the end of the age" (Matt. 28:18–20).

Are we to imagine that Jesus would have made this tremendous statement if there was no real prospect of success? Are we to think that he would have talked about bringing the whole world to the obedience of faith if the entire operation was bound to fail in the end? Yet this is what many Christians believe today. And they even think that they are being very devout when they believe it. But what does the Bible say? It says, *"Then comes the end, when He delivers the kingdom to God the Father, when He puts an end to all rule and all authority and power. For He must reign till He has put all enemies under His feet"* (1 Cor. 15:24–25). It is this optimistic eschatology that we find in the Heidelberg Catechism.

The kingdom of God, which is now under the authority of Jesus Christ, does not come with observation. It cannot be seen in the way that one can see the United States of America or Great Britain. No, it comes by the power of the Spirit of God in connection with gospel preaching. This is one of the keys of the kingdom. The other is the faithful exercise of church discipline. We know this because Jesus said that he was giving the keys that lock and unlock the kingdom to the officers of his church. And we know—from the book of Acts, where we see these men in action—that it was by means of these two things that the early church began the conquest of the world. Sometimes—where *we* happen to be—the progress of this conquest of the nations may seem quite slow and discouraging. Indeed, in a given nation, things may indeed go from good to bad and from bad to worse. We believe that this has been happening, in recent decades, in much of the Western world. Yet when we look at a world map showing the areas where there are faithful Christian churches today, and then compare that with a map showing the situation in the year 500—or 1000—or 1500—it will be readily apparent that God's kingdom *is* coming, more and more. And it is coming because God *is* ruling his people, more and more, by his Spirit and Word. Whenever God sends reformation to his church, and it again becomes the salt of the earth, there is a defeat of the forces of Satan and an advance of the kingdom of God. Every conspiracy that man raises up against God is, in the end, a failure. A generation ago we saw the rise—and then the fall—of the horrible Nazi ideology. More recently we have seen the fall of communism. These kingdoms of the world have been destroyed because Jesus Christ really does have the power and authority—the resources, as we would call them today—to bring about their destruction.

Christians today need, perhaps as much as anything else, to recover the kind of faith in their risen Lord that begets great expectations. If we do not expect to win, it follows that we will not fight very well. This became very clear to me during World War II. The U.S. Government provided training films to better prepare its fighting men psychologically. Sometimes this is called "brainwashing." But it was not brainwashing in the sense of destroying a person's ability to think for himself. These films simply presented the evidence in order to enable a thinking person to decide on the facts. The factual evidence was to the effect that the Allied forces had a tremendous advantage in resources, industrial capacity, and manpower. When we saw these films we realized that we were going to win—even if it had to be in the long run. It is the same with the cause of Christ. He has infinite resources, whereas Satan does not. And he has given these resources (the Word and the Spirit) to his church. It is therefore certain that his kingdom, not the evil empire, is going to prevail in history. That is why we are to pray this petition.

QUESTIONS ON THE LESSON

1. What is the commonly accepted idea concerning the kingdom of God?
2. At what points is this common view contradicted by the apostle Paul in 1 Corinthians 15:24–25?
3. What resources does the church have that far surpass those of the Devil?
4. Why is it important to have a proper view of eschatology?

QUESTIONS FOR STUDY AND DISCUSSION

1. List some significant ways in which Christianity has affected the world and its cultures.
2. What passages of Scripture are often used to support the doctrine of a future Antichrist who will rule the whole world?

3. In what passages of Scripture is the term *antichrist* actually used? What is its meaning there?
4. Explain *"The meek . . . shall inherit the earth"* (Matt. 5:5) and *"The promise that he would be the heir of the world was not to Abraham or to his seed through the law"* (Rom. 4:13).

LORD'S DAY 49

SCRIPTURE READINGS: *Philippians 2:12–18; Colossians 3:1–4:6*

124. Q. What is the third petition?

A. *Thy will be done, as in heaven, so on earth.* That is: grant that we and all men may renounce our own will, and without any gainsaying obey Thy will, which alone is good; that so every one may discharge the duties of his office and calling as willingly and faithfully as the angels in heaven.

It is right here that we see how God's kingdom comes. It comes as we—together with all other believers—are brought by the Spirit and the Word of God to the obedience of faith. This, it will be noted, is both an individual and a corporate thing. This means that each of us must do this personally and really. But it also means that we do not do it alone, but with others. This is the way it is in heaven. No angel acts in an autonomous way, as if there were no hierarchy (higher and lower ranks) among the angels. But we know that there is a hierarchy among the angels, because some of them are called archangels. This means that some angels have greater authority than others, which implies that the angels having greater authority receive respect from those having less. In this there is a real analogy with our human obedience. Our obedience to God must be personal, yes, but it must also be corporate. For example, the Bible requires children to obey their parents (Eph. 6:1). This is the way that children do the will of God. Similarly, we in the church are to obey our leaders and submit to their authority (Heb. 13:17). It is understood, of course, that this applies only to leaders who are themselves faithful to the Scriptures. But if they are, our submission to them is a part of our submission to Jesus. So the individualism and autonomy that is so common today is completely contrary to Scripture.

Many Christians today belong to churches that are no longer faithful. They may even realize it, but then say that it does not affect them because they still believe the Bible. This is erroneous thinking, because part of our obedience to Christ is to belong to a church that enables us to obey him together. When I belong to a denomination that is faithful to the Bible, it means that my offerings are serving the cause of Christ and not the cause of the Devil.

The same thing is involved in all aspects of life, and we need to be more conscious of it. For example, it is the will of God for me to bring up my children in the nurture and admonition of the Lord. But how can I do that if I turn them over—six or eight hours a day—to teachers who undermine and contradict that Christian nurture? It is imperative for Christians to become much more conscious of their corporate involvement. We ought to do much more than we have done in the past—in a collective or corporate way—so that we can really do the will of God in every aspect of life. What we need, in other words, is not just Christians. No, we also need Christian schools, Christian labor unions, Christian political parties, and so on. The more we learn to do this, the more we will see this petition answered.

QUESTIONS ON THE LESSON

1. What can we learn from the angels about doing God's will?
2. What is a basic error in the argument of believers who remain in unfaithful denominations?
3. Can we do the will of God without obeying human authorities? Why?
4. How can we act in a corporate or communal way in order to obey Jesus?

QUESTIONS FOR STUDY AND DISCUSSION

1. Sometimes one hears the question, "How can I find God's will for my life?" What is meant by this question? How would you answer it?
2. The answer given by the Catechism to this question involves hard work. We must reject our own wills, obey God, and carry out the

work he calls us to do. How would you answer the charge that such a view of the Christian life amounts to legalistic salvation by works?

3. How would you answer someone who says that the will of God is not to work but to rest in God's work, to wait quietly while he does mighty things, to let go of our attempts to accomplish his work and let him do it?

LORD'S DAY 50

SCRIPTURE READINGS: *Deuteronomy 8;*
Psalm 145:14–21; Matthew 6:25–33

125. Q. What is the fourth petition?

   A. *Give us this day our daily bread.* That is: be pleased to provide for all our bodily need, that we may thereby acknowledge Thee to be the only fountain of all good, and
   that without Thy blessing neither our care and labor nor
   Thy gifts can profit us; and, therefore, that we may with-
   draw our trust from all creatures and place it alone in Thee.

There is still a measure of uncertainty as to the meaning of the Greek
word *(epiousion)* translated "daily." It occurs nowhere else in the Bible
(except in Luke's parallel version of this prayer) and has been found
only once in ancient writings outside of the Bible. In such cases trans-
lators have to do some educated guess work. John Chrysostom, the
great Greek preacher, took it to mean "necessary for existence, or
needful for life." Some have taken it to mean "for today, or for the
daily ration." Others have taken it to mean "for tomorrow, or for the
future." Some have even taken the whole phrase to refer, at least primarily, to "the bread of life"—in other words, the believer's spiritual
bread. But when all is said and done, there is still an element of uncertainty as to its precise meaning. And this may well be the design of
the Holy Spirit, who inspired these writers. Since we do not know the
exact usage of this term among the ancients, we are constrained to
stick to the things that *are* certain. When we do this, it does not diminish the importance of this petition. To the contrary, it rather mag-
nifies its importance.

And what are the certainties? One is the fact that bread always was, and still is today, "the staff of life" (to quote a proverbial saying). On the well-known principle of using one particular example to stand for an entire class, bread clearly stands for what is essential. In this petition, in other words, we are instructed by Jesus to ask God for the most basic things that we require for our very existence. Now this could be the bread for today. It could be the bread for tomorrow. But whichever it is, the main thing is perfectly clear. We are to humbly ask God to grant us the very necessities of life—and from this we can make a deduction.

The deduction is that we do not deserve even the most basic things that we must have to sustain us. Yet how common it is today for people to take these things for granted—to maintain, for example, that the government owes all of us a living. What a radical thing it is, in contrast to this, when someone today says what the patriarch Jacob once said—thousands of years ago—*"I am not worthy of the least of all the mercies . . . which You have shown Your servant"* (Gen. 32:10). And that is not all.

Another deduction that clearly follows is that even when it comes to the basic necessities of life, it is only by the unmerited favor of God that we receive them. This is why we are to be content with the portion God gives us. This does not mean that we should not work diligently to improve our condition. But it does mean that we are not to murmur and complain if we have less than someone else does, as if God had withheld something that we had coming! No, the truth is that even if we only have enough—with nothing to spare—we must still say that we have received, out of the mercy and kindness of God, what we did not merit.

Finally, in praying this fourth request, we are taught that we must learn to put our trust in God, and in God alone, even for the most basic and necessary things of this life. It was in recognition of this implication that a wise man named Agur prayed these words: *"Give me neither poverty nor riches—feed me with the food You prescribe for me; lest I be full and deny You, and say, 'Who is the LORD?' Or lest I be poor and steal, and profane the name of my God"* (Prov. 30:8–9). Jesus said that it is particularly hard for a rich man to enter into the kingdom of heaven. This may be the source of the difficulty: the rich man has so much that he no longer feels himself to be dependent. But note that when the poor man steals, he also renounces—in effect—what this part of the Lord's Prayer is teaching. Let us ask the Lord, then, to help us pray this request with the wisdom of Agur.

QUESTIONS ON THE LESSON

1. What does the word *daily (epiousion)* mean?
2. What does the word *bread* stand for in this request? How does Proverbs 30:8 help us in being certain of this?
3. State one or two principles that we can deduce from this request.
4. Why did Agur pray that the Lord would make him neither too rich nor too poor? Are these dangers different, or are they really the same?

QUESTIONS FOR STUDY AND DISCUSSION

1. Even believers do not always trust the Lord for their needs. Give some examples from your own experience that show a lack of trust in the Lord. In these examples, what or whom was being trusted instead of God?
2. Since God is our Creator, doesn't he have an obligation to provide for our needs? Explain.
3. Since God is the one who provides for us, is there any need for us to work for or worry about the things we need?

LORD'S DAY 51

SCRIPTURE READINGS: *Matthew 18:15–35;*
Luke 15:11–32; Ephesians 4:30–5:2

126. Q. What is the fifth petition?

A. *And forgive us our debts, as we also have forgiven our debtors.*
That is: be pleased, for the sake of Christ's blood, not to
impute to us, miserable sinners, any of our transgressions,
nor the evil which always cleaves to us; as we also find this
witness of Thy grace in us that it is our full purpose heartily
to forgive our neighbor.

It is worthy of note that this petition was the one that Jesus com-
mented on right after he taught his disciples this prayer. He said: *"For*
if you forgive men their trespasses, your heavenly Father will also forgive
you. But if you do not forgive men their trespasses, neither will your Father
forgive your trespasses" (Matt. 6:14–15). But how, it may be asked, can
God's forgiveness of us be dependent upon our forgiveness of others?
Does God wait to see if we will truly forgive others before he truly for-
gives us? No, of course not. The Bible is full of proof that God's forgiveness is freely granted to any and all who repent of their sin and believe in Jesus. And God does not wait for us to do some good thing
first, so that he can then do good to us. No, God treats us—when we
repent and believe—just as the father treated his son in the parable of
the prodigal son.

Well, then, does this mean that God may forgive our sins and then
take back that forgiveness later if we refuse to forgive others? The answer to this is yes—in one sense. When we are received into the fellowship of the church of God, we are promised the gift of forgiveness.

But, like all the great promises of God, this one is conditional, too. God does not say, "You are a forgiven person, and so now you can live any way you please, and forgiveness will never be taken from you." No, what God says is that we must live a life of gratitude in obedience to his commandments. And one of those commandments is that we should forgive others as we ourselves have been forgiven. And so—as in the famous parable of the ungrateful servant—if we are not willing to forgive others who sin against us, then God will withhold that (conditionally) promised forgiveness that we expected from him.

To put it a different way, we have no right whatever to think that we are forgiven by God unless we "find this witness of Thy grace in us that it is our full purpose heartily to forgive our neighbor." Any other combination of things would involve a complete contradiction, the kind of contradiction that has no place in God's kingdom. One could as well speak of a round square, or an empty fullness, as speak of an unforgiving Christian. There may be, and probably are, many who are unforgiving and yet *called* Christians. But there are no *real* Christians who are unforgiving, because the same God who grants us forgiveness as a free gift also grants us the free gift of his Holy Spirit. And when the Holy Spirit dwells in our hearts, renewing them, it is not possible for us to remain unforgiving. Indeed, this is one of the ways that we can test ourselves to know whether or not we have grounds for assurance.

QUESTIONS ON THE LESSON

1. Does this request imply that God waits to forgive us until we first forgive others?
2. Is it possible for a Christian to receive—and then lose—God's forgiveness?
3. Why is it impossible for a man to be truly forgiven by God and remain unforgiving himself?
4. When we know that we are forgiving, what can we conclude?

QUESTIONS FOR STUDY AND DISCUSSION

1. Is it enough to forgive a person seven times? How about 490 times (Matt. 18:21–22)? Explain.

2. Did the Lord really mean for us to forgive a repentant brother seven times on the same day? Explain Luke 17:3–4.
3. What is involved in forgiving? Does it mean forgetting? Does it mean never bringing the matter up again? Does it mean acting as though nothing had happened?

LORD'S DAY 52

SCRIPTURE READINGS: *John 16:7–11;
James 2:12–18; 1 John 2:15–17; 4:1–6*

127. Q. What is the sixth petition?

A. *And bring us not into temptation, but deliver us from the evil one.* That is: since we are so weak in ourselves that we cannot stand a moment, and besides, since our sworn enemies, the devil, the world, and our own flesh, cease not to assault us, be pleased to preserve and strengthen us by the power of Thy Holy Spirit, that we may not succumb in this spiritual warfare but always offer strong resistance, till at last we obtain a complete victory.

Two things need emphasis in this section of the Catechism's exposition of the Lord's Prayer. First, it in no way minimizes the magnitude of the conflict between the believer and the trinity of evil—the world, the flesh (that is, our own sinful nature), and the Devil. The biblical view is that we—in and of ourselves—could never stand up against these things. Even the greatest men of God had to fight a difficult battle, and we could say that they won that battle with nothing to spare. Yet, in the second place, the Catechism does say that we must resist "till at last we obtain a complete victory." After all, as the apostle John truly said, *"He who is in you [i.e., the Holy Spirit] is greater than he who is in the world"* (1 John 4:4). And it is precisely because both of these things are true that we must learn to ask the Lord to grant us the strength that comes from the Holy Spirit. On the one hand, as Jesus said, without him we can do nothing (John 15:5). On the other hand, as the apostle Paul said, we can do all things through Christ who strengthens us (Phil. 4:13).

You will notice that there are two parts to this sixth request. First, there is a negative part: we ask God not to bring us into temptation. Here we acknowledge God's absolute sovereignty over us. We can pray this way only if we know that nothing is outside God's control. The book of Job shows this clearly. Every calamity that came upon Job was brought about through the agency of Satan. But Satan could only go as far as God permitted him to go. This being true, there is no escape from the thought implied in the first half of this request—that if we are to be tempted, then it will be God (who controls all things) who brings us into that temptation.

If we rightly recognize our own weakness, then, we will always pray that God in his mercy would be pleased to spare us from being tempted. Had Peter, for example, understood his own weakness, he would have asked to be kept from denying his Lord, instead of boasting that he would never do such a thing. It was for this very reason that Jesus warned him to pray—so that he would not enter into temptation (Luke 22:40).

Because of our weakness, we ought to ask the Lord not to lead us into temptation. But, having done this, if it is the will of God to bring us into temptation, we can then go on to ask the Lord to deliver us from "the evil." We put these words in quotation marks because we are uncertain as to the exact meaning of the original text at this point. Did Jesus mean "the evil one," that is, Satan? Or did he mean "the evil thing"—in whatever form it might come to us, whether from the world, the flesh, or the Devil? We are not quite sure, but in the final analysis it makes little difference. All evil is somehow related to the prince of the power of darkness. Yet the good news is that we are going to win a complete victory over that prince and his whole kingdom.

There is nothing in the whole Bible to justify a foolish presumption, such as Peter had when he boasted that he would never deny his Lord. But, at the same time, it is just as true that there is no justification for a pessimistic outlook on the part of the believer. Paul says that God is going to complete the good work that he has begun in us (Phil. 1:5). He also assured the Christians at Rome that *"the God of peace will crush Satan under your feet shortly"* (Rom. 16:20). When we understand both of these things and learn to pray according to the meaning of this sixth request, we will find the help we need to win the victory to which the Lord calls us.

QUESTIONS ON THE LESSON

1. Why did Jesus put these two things together in one request?
2. Does God bring us into temptation?
3. What are the three principal enemies of the believer?
4. What are the two main truths implied in this request?

QUESTIONS FOR STUDY AND DISCUSSION

1. How can the Bible teach that God brings us into temptation and yet that God tempts no man?
2. What assurance do we have that God's people, in spite of their weakness, will not be overcome, individually or corporately, by the Evil One?
3. What implications for the Christian warfare can be drawn from John 16:7–11?

Lord's Day 52—Continued

SCRIPTURE READINGS: *Psalm 115;*
Romans 11:33–36; Jude 24–25

128. Q. How do you conclude your prayer?

A. *For thine is the kingdom, and the power, and the glory for ever.*
That is: all this we ask of Thee because Thou, as our King
who hast power over all things, art both willing and able
to give us all good, and that thereby not we but Thy holy
Name may be glorified for ever.

129. Q. What does the word *Amen* signify?

A. *Amen* signifies: it shall truly and surely be; for my prayer
is more certainly heard of God than I feel in my heart that
I desire these things of Him.

It now seems clear that the concluding words of the Lord's Prayer, as we
call it, were not part of the original text of the Bible. We say this because some ancient manuscripts lack them entirely, while others have
longer and shorter versions. The reason for this is probably that the
church, from very early times, used this prayer in worship and felt the
need for some such ending for liturgical purposes. This ending may have
been composed, as some have suggested, using 1 Chronicles 29:11–13
as a basis. In any event, there is nothing in this concluding summation
that is contrary to the sense and meaning of the prayer itself or to the
rest of the Bible. In fact, the very content of the prayer itself implies
what is contained in this conclusion. For how could we make the six
great requests contained in the body of the prayer if God were not the
all-powerful ruler who is able to give us all that is good? And how could

we presume to ask these things if we did not know that to do so is for his glory? In other words, we could never ask these things if we did not believe that God is able to do what we ask, understand that these things are to his glory, and know that it shall be so forever!

The true believer gives a hearty "amen" to God. That is, he expresses the willing agreement of his own mind and heart with the revealed mind and will of the heavenly Father. And the better we know this prayer that Jesus taught his disciples, the more strongly we can say it. We again remind the reader that this prayer is like a model house. It is not here so that we can live in it. It is here so we will have a plan for a house we can live in. Jesus' main purpose in giving this prayer to his disciples was to give them a model for their own prayers. His words *"In this manner, therefore, pray"* (Matt. 6:9) make that clear. As we learn to understand the content of these six requests, and agree wholeheartedly with their sense and meaning, we can also say the hearty "amen" at the conclusion.

QUESTIONS ON THE LESSON

1. Why is it doubtful that the well-known conclusion to the Lord's Prayer was originally in the Bible?
2. Does this mean that we should not use it? Why?
3. What do we need before we can properly say "Amen"?

QUESTIONS FOR STUDY AND DISCUSSION

1. Since God delights to hear the prayer of his children, and since he is able to give them all they need, why does he at times withhold what they need?
2. Because of our weakness, it is often true that we pray for good things but don't really desire them as we ought. In such cases, does God still accept our prayer? Give scriptural support for your answer.

INDEX OF SCRIPTURE